Reunion

MONTANA BRED SERIES
BOOK 2

LINDA BRADLEY

Akin House Publishing

DEDICATION

For Roni Hall
who inspires me to kiss life in the face!

ACKNOWLEDGMENTS

Thank you to the readers. Your support and interaction inspire me to write. Once upon a time, Montana seemed like a dream. Now, it's a regular part of my world and calls to me much like it does to the characters of the 617 Ranch. There's nothing sweeter than the scent of sage and wild-flowers on a summer day when I'm riding a horse in the mountains.

Thank you to the wonderful Julie Sturgeon for editing *Reunion*. I appreciate your expertise, suggestions, and support in shaping Chloe and Brook's story.

Thank you to my writing pals, the Babes. You're my go-to when I need beta readers and brainstorming sessions to continue the writing process.

Thank you to Nan Rowe for another gorgeous cover. Your impeccable design and eye for color captures this story in a single photo.

Thank you to the MMRWA members and Greater Detroit Romance Writers for your support and friendship.

Thank you to my family for the unconditional

love and support. Without you, the journey wouldn't be nearly as adventurous or rewarding. You are my heart!

Maggie's Fork in the Road
(Montana Bound Series Book 2)

"I loved the first book in the series. This is women's fiction with a delightful voice and cast of characters. Maggie continues her story with the same eccentric cast of characters and a new adventure to grasp. If she can just let go of her fears. I love the 'feel' of this book."
—Susan B. James, *Maybe This Time*, a Raven Award for Contemporary

"Author Linda Bradley shows us another side…a stronger side…of a heroine I already admired. It could only get better from there."
—Nancy Fraser, *Notes from a Romantic's Heart*

Maggie's Montana
(Montana Bound Series Book 3)

"Guaranteed to touch your heart. . .Maggie's Montana is a must read for women's fiction lovers. Linda Bradley's writing sings in this beautifully crafted, warm and funny story about the bonds of love and friendship."
—Kim Boykin, author of *The Wisdom of Hair* and *Palmetto Moon*

"Linda Bradley's distinct voice draws you in as her misfit cast of characters wrap around your heart and take you home."
—Roni Hall, author of *Montana Wild*

A Montana Bound Christmas:
Ho, Ho, Home for the Holidays!
(Montana Bound Series Book 4)

"What fun! From the first chapter to the last, this story is a like a warm hug. Linda Bradley weaves the different worlds of each of the characters together in a rich tapestry that mirrors the story line itself. This could easily become a beloved holiday movie classic."

—Annette Rochelle Aben, #1 best seller

"If you like your holiday romance with a lot of feel-good emotions, you'll really enjoy this continuation of the Montana Bound series."

—Nancy Fraser, award-winning author

"Ms. Bradley has produced another delightful read...a Christmas gift for all of us."

—Joanne Guidoccio, author of *Too Many Women in the Room*

"If you've read the Montana Bound series, this is a welcome addition, and if you haven't – you can read it as a standalone, but to get the full impact of what these characters have been through, start at the beginning, *Maggie's Way*."

—Cyrene Olson, Uncaged Book Reviews

Unbranded
(Montana Bred Series Book 1)

"You know, Chloe—life is thorny like the rosebush you planted on the ridge in memory of your granddad, and sometimes the thorniest bushes have the best blooms."

Maggie took the pressed yellow rose preserved in a delicate white frame from the tub. Matt had picked the flower from the rosebush planted on the ridge in memory of my grandpa, and had given it to me the day I'd gotten pregnant. The one time we'd let down our guards and explored our relationship beyond friendship led to unexpected parenthood. Despite taking precautions, we'd been left with not one surprise, but two. Vulnerability was a slippery slope, and these babies had a heap of good people waiting to welcome them.

"I don't want to end up like my parents," I muttered under my breath.

"You didn't cause the rift between them," Maggie said.

"Maybe not, but I *am* part of the equation." I leafed through my riding awards. Gravity tugged at the corners of my mouth.

I went to the window, opened it, and took in the view of the mountains, endless blue skies the background to my playground. The breeze left butterfly kisses upon my cheeks.

"When's your mom coming?" Glad asked.

"She'll book a flight once the babies arrive. She's already sent two boxes of clothing for them. Come look in the babies' room. She also sent two matching toddler lounge chairs."

"They're so cute. The wooden legs look like logs, and the patchwork quilt fabric is adorable." Glad took a woolly lamb stuffed animal from the shelf and set it on one of the lofty cushions.

Maggie rested her hands on her mother's shoulders. "Your mom is a special breed." She took a deep breath. "You do know there's a chance she may not come."

Remembering the times in my youth when my mother was a no-show or left me behind without saying goodbye, I ignored Maggie's comment and her concerned expression. This time would be different.

"I'm hungry." I hung the framed rose on a nail I'd secured above the dresser. The keepsake was a sweet reminder of everything dear to me.

"We ate pancakes and bacon less than an hour ago, then you finished off the hot pickle and beef sandwich from yesterday. And Glad brought leftovers."

"I can't help it. I want ice cream."

"Eat the rolls. They're fresh and gooey. Ice cream is for after dinner," Glad said.

"Come on. I don't want to eat alone. I won't have an excuse for cravings after the babies are born. And don't worry about the cinnamon rolls. I'll take care of them later." I waddled out of the room and went downstairs. Maggie and Glad followed. "You can visit any time you like. I hope Dad has more stories to tell me about this place."

"I'm sure he does. It'll be like opening a favorite book you haven't read in a long time. I'll take photos after we get the rest of your things moved in. I took pictures prior to the renovation. I'm making a keepsake for your dad. He'll get a kick out of seeing his childhood home spruced up. The refinished floors glow. Makes me want to take off my boots and slide across them in my stocking feet. The renovation delay was worth it." Maggie ran her hand across the rounded cap of the thick newel post at the foot of the staircase that covered a compartment where my grandparents had placed the original floor plan of the timber house.

"Look what I saved." I showed Maggie the pencil markings showing my dad's height until the age of sixteen on the doorjamb inside the closet at the bottom of the steps. "I'd like to continue the tradition. I'm so glad Grandpa and Grandma built this place after they got married. I love the new house Grandpa built before Dad and I came here, but this one is extra special. Just being here gives me the warm fuzzies."

Maggie fingered the marks from when my dad was a toddler, then wandered into the kitchen and came back with a pencil. "It's hard to imagine your father being knee-high. Stand against the doorjamb. I'll mark your height."

"But I'm an adult."

"Do it for me. Please."

I did as she said. When I stepped away, she wrote the date, my age, and *Chloe's first day home.*

"It is home, isn't it?" I peered into the living room. The timbers soaked in the warm light from outdoors. The fieldstone hearth had been laid by my grandpa, and the horseshoes tacked to the hand-hewn mantel were shinier than ever. "Can I call you tonight if I get lonely? I've never had my own place."

"Yes, you can call. But you'll be fine. What do you say we get the kitchen under control in between bites?"

Glad went outside for another load. "There are two calves out here," she called through the screen door.

I picked up a stack of broken-down boxes in the mudroom, followed Glad, and loaded them into the back of Maggie's SUV. Calf 311 lifted her nose from the sweet grass as I read her companion's tag.

"Nice to see you, 313," I said.

The calves' black noses and onyx-colored eyes against their white hides resembled one of Mom's stunning designs. Samson, our lazy bulldog, stood between them. I stroked 311's head. "You're getting to be a big girl." She sniffed my belly, and the babies responded with a kick.

Maggie hurried down the deck stairs. "Seven months, weaned, and naughty. Wonder if the guys know they're out again?"

"They can visit me any time."

Samson barked, waddled over, made his way up the stairs, and curled up in the sun.

Maggie picked up the magazine I'd left on the deck rail and skimmed the pages featuring my mom.

I rubbed my belly and caught my breath. "Whoa, that felt like a tidal wave. I reckon the babies are anxious to meet the animals." I hoped they were excited to be part of the world I'd told them about while lying in bed watching ribbons of moonlight paint the ceiling when I couldn't sleep.

"You love your animals as much as your people." Maggie took a seat on the bottom step next to her mom.

"Not to mention these babies." I took cattle cube treats from my pocket and fed them to the calves.

"And those babies are gonna love you as much as those calves you've coddled since birth." Glad pointed to a fringed woolen shawl and dog-eared the page of the magazine. "Your momma and Hermione make for a fierce team."

"I'm going to order the straw cowboy hat with the wide striped hatband. I also like that embroidered tunic belted in silver and turquoise." I smoothed down my shirt looking forward to the day my belly bump, big enough to balance my dinner plate on, would be gone.

"Your mother thrives on business." Creases appeared at the corners of Maggie's eyes.

"What if we're more alike than I think?" I made my way onto the deck and sat down in the Adirondack chair. "I gotta quit sitting here. Getting up is gonna be an issue."

The phone rang in the kitchen. I tried to move but couldn't propel my weight forward from the downward slant of the seat.

"Help me up, please." I squirmed, trying to get traction beneath my boots.

Maggie stood and offered me her hands. She

pulled, wrinkled the bridge of her nose, and planted her right foot against the chair leg for leverage.

"You're funny." I scooted to the edge and pushed myself up. "I'll answer the phone. You keep an eye on the calves, Harpo."

"I'll shut the gate to the drive. But something tells me they're not going far."

Glad held the door for me.

I hurried through the mudroom and into the kitchen to grab the landline receiver. "Hello."

"Miguel, make sure the McCarthy meeting is moved to Tuesday, and make sure the mock-ups make it to the art department before three. Heads will roll if they're late, and I don't think being fired is on your agenda today. If Suzanne calls, I'm busy."

I hoped my mother would exhaust that familiar tone before her arrival.

"Hi, Mom."

She cleared her voice with a heavy sigh.

"What's wrong?"

"Good help is so hard to find."

"Don't I know it. The nanny I had lined up left us for a banker with a time-share in Boca Raton. Starting over stinks, but I've got another woman interested in the position and scheduled for an interview."

"Did you receive the organic soaps, lotions, shampoos, and terry towels with the cows on them for the babies? I hope you like the bath salts and candles."

"Not yet. And, Mom, if I sat in the tub, I'd need a crane to get me out. You don't have to send gifts. The chairs for the twins came yesterday. Growing into them will take some time." I couldn't bring myself to tell her that she was all I needed.

"Call me if you go into labor before I get there. I'm looking forward to seeing you tomorrow."

"Tomorrow? You said you'd fly in *after* the babies came."

"I figured you'd need my help getting the house organized, and the babies will be here any day now."

Maggie and Glad came inside.

I listened to Mom ramble on about getting the best plane ticket she could.

"I arrive at noon, and I've rented a car. Everything should be set on your end. I secured a sporty ride. No sedans or trucks and nothing that makes me look like a senior," she said.

"Tomorrow though?" I drummed my fingers on the cool granite counter.

"Batten down the hatches," Glad whispered with a giggle.

Maggie opened and closed cupboards, taking inventory.

Mom continued to tell me what she'd packed and the prognosis of her hair in a different climate. I held the phone near Maggie, who smiled as she made a shopping list. I took the pen from her and wrote *patience, the economy size*, then pressed the receiver back to my ear.

"Mom." I swallowed hard. The babies kicked with the spurs I was sure they'd be born with.

"I hope the airlines don't lose my luggage. I'm bringing an empty suitcase. Can't wait to go shopping. Have you worn the studded cowboy boots I sent you for your birthday, Chloe?"

"Not yet. I'm waiting for the right occasion. It doesn't seem right to wear them while mucking out stalls and wading through mud."

"Nonsense. Wear the boots, Chloe, or I'll buy them in every color."

"Forget the boots, Mom. Just get here and hang." The babies induced another sharp pang, and I rested my hand on my lower back.

"I'm looking forward to meeting Matt and seeing the ranch. I bet your granddaddy's spread hasn't changed a bit."

"See you tomorrow, Mom." I hung up. "We need the living room and kitchen furniture from the old barn loft before she gets here. I'll call Dad and tell him I've marked the pieces I want. Do you mind going to the grocery store alone?"

"Not at all," Maggie replied. "Looks like you're getting what you wanted."

"I am. It really is time." I fanned my cheeks. "I've got this."

CHAPTER 3

"**M**OM'S COMING EARLY. This is a new tactic." I got out the huckleberry ice cream.

"This will give you time to yourselves before the babies come," Maggie said. "I thought you didn't have any food in the fridge."

"I nabbed it from the main house after breakfast. The animals aren't the only ones who like treats." I took three bowls from the open moving box. "I need this now as much as I need the guys to get the furniture from the loft in Grandpa's barn. Whiskey isn't an option. Everything's getting a bit too real."

"It will be for me if your head keeps spinning," Glad said. "I'm taking the towels upstairs, and I'll be organizing the bathroom. And while you were on the phone, there was a delivery at the front door."

"Must be the bath goodies Mom mentioned."

"That, and something else," Glad answered. "The *something else* is in the living room. You won't miss it. You know where to find me if you need me." She growled and shook her head.

I scooped ice cream into my bowl. "The house isn't done. The babies aren't here. What if Mom wants to be in the delivery room?"

Ice cream splattered on the counter. Maggie wiped up the sticky residue and returned the carton to the fridge.

"Leave it out. I may need seconds."

"We don't have time."

The hurried, quiet indulgence created a silence between us, not the awkward kind but the kind that held you close when you were with a good friend, the soothing kind, the kind brought about by unconditional love. The kind of silence that meant something because someone was spending all their energy on holding your heart when words wouldn't change the situation.

The kind of silence my mother and I hadn't shared before I got on a plane and came home early after telling her our relationship should be more important than her work.

"There's always the path to Trout's house. He cleared it just for you." Maggie put the dirty dishes in the dishwasher.

"You're the second person who's mentioned that today. What if Mom's best isn't good enough?"

"It's not *her* best you should be focused on. You didn't doubt your decision when you invited her, so why start now?" Maggie wiped down the counter. "Look, right now you're confined to basic everyday life, and that's challenging enough. Not to mention, you've got two babies who are so attached to their momma, they're holding out for every last minute with you." Maggie touched the silver charm on my necklace. "There isn't a day I can remember that you haven't worn this. It's only natural to want your mom, especially now."

"I do. I won't let myself give up on her again."

"I know you won't. You're a good daughter, Chloe."

I stood, then sat back down when my belly cramped. I gripped the edge of the table and took a deep breath.

"Are you okay?"

When the pain subsided, I noted the time on the kitchen clock.

"Chloe, answer me."

"I'm not ready for them. What if I can't handle the babies? We don't have a nanny. What if I can't handle my mother?" My mother's absence from my childhood crept into the thoughts I'd agreed to put behind me. As hard as I tried to forget, the invisible scars didn't always feel so invisible.

"You'll handle your mom and the babies just fine. You'll also find a nanny," Maggie said.

"As usual, you're the calm one." I fanned away the flash of heat in my cheeks. "There's safety in numbers. Right?"

"Yes—there's safety in numbers. We're in this together, including me and everyone else on this ranch. Let it go, girl." Maggie wiped her hands on a black-and-white spotted dishtowel that read You Are Moo-velous. She pointed to the embroidery. "The cows have spoken."

A familiar hand kneaded my shoulder. I peered up into Dad's brooding gaze. His left temple twitched. "How long have you been standing there?"

"Long enough. You've got your own place now. Your mother is welcome. If you two get along, great. If not—move on. Don't let the past dictate the future, sweetheart. Nothing good comes from that. Don't let your mom knock you off your horse, and remember, you're wearing your big girl pants. I believe that's what you refer to them as."

I smoothed down the linen tunic I wore over my stretchy denim. "All day, every day." I wrapped my paisley bandanna around my head, tied it in back, then pushed it to my forehead.

"Take one step at a time, and if you feel yourself taking a stride backward—simmer down and take a deep breath," he said.

"I will."

Maggie tied her hair back and tugged at the front of her plaid shirt. She exchanged glances with my dad as they waited for a break in the drama. Between the two of them, the well of patience ran deep, but I knew they had their limits.

"You ready to see what's waiting for you in the living room?" Maggie smiled.

"Sure. Let's take that next step." I led the way.

Glad came downstairs. Dad chuckled as he scratched his whiskery chin.

"Oh brother. Do I look like the bearskin rug kind of girl? I don't think so. What am I gonna do with it? What was Mom thinking? That snarling face is what nightmares are made of—frightening." I snapped a photo of the intimidating rug with my phone and sent it to my mom. I zoomed in on the bear's fierce expression and sent that picture, too. "Can the guys bring the furniture from the old barn so I can send her a picture of a full living room? Please."

"The men who delivered the rug said it was faux," Glad said.

"Sure looks real," Maggie whispered. "Those teeth are wicked."

"The eyes, and it's so big." Glad shivered.

"Good thing it's a down day in the pasture. I'll see if the crew is done checking the herds. I'm sure they'll help move the furniture. Can't wait to see my mom's table and chairs in the kitchen again. Maybe you should send that picture, too." Dad tugged at the brim of his cowboy hat. "Chloe, you okay?"

"Sure, Dad. Just wondering where to put this rug after Mom leaves."

THE MANIC RUSH to get the house in order didn't mute my ticking clock. My back ached, and I internalized everything I was and wasn't to my mother. Leaving the past behind me was easier said than done. I was ready to kick off my boots and lie down, but not before finishing my to-do list.

Dad, Matt, Tristan, and Silas brought the furniture from the barn. They placed the leather sofa, once belonging to Maggie, beside the faux bear rug Mom had sent. Matt and Silas had rotated the rug, making its grisly stare point toward my office and away from anyone entering the living room. The sofa's dimpled leather complemented the wood floors, and I found comfort in having a piece of Maggie with me day and night.

"The sofa looks great," Maggie said. "So glad we kept it. You sure you don't want to buy a new one? I'll go shopping with you."

"Nope, don't want to go shopping. It's perfect. Brings back good memories." I folded the woolen throw woven with chocolate and salmon hues Maggie had given me for a birthday present last August, and set it on the trunk in the corner. "The guys will be relieved to be done here. They'd rather be riding or tinkering in the barn. Can't say I blame them."

Maggie sat at one end of the sofa, and I sat at the other. I propped my feet on the leather ottoman large enough for a couple of lanky hounds. The sparsely decorated living room still didn't appear complete enough to detour my mother from adding additional touches.

"Mom will say I don't have enough furniture." I took in the rich earthy tones and sank deeper into the cushy sofa. I smiled, imagining myself snuggled beneath a warm blanket on a cold evening in front of the fireplace. "I hope Mom likes it here."

"She will, and you know my philosophy. Fill it with memories." Maggie glanced around the room, her green eyes bright as ever.

"Thank goodness the mattress was delivered for the spare bed." I blew stray strands of hair away from my face.

"If you need anything, you know where to find me. You're welcome to eat with us and the crew." Maggie adjusted her strawberry blonde ponytail.

"Thank you. What if these babies are a handful? Two babies—of course they'll be a handful."

"Like I said before—you'll do a fine job dealing with whatever comes your way. I was nervous before I had Bradley, too. Can't believe he's forty-one and in a serious relationship. Time flies, dear girl. Wish he lived closer. Boston's too far away." Maggie stood.

"Thanks for letting me have the queen-sized sleigh bed and dresser from the main house. I've always loved it. Makes me think of fairy tales and magic carpet rides," I said.

"No problem. Now I have an empty room to play with. Trout set up the cribs, and you know where to find what you don't have."

"Sure do."

"How'd Mom do organizing the guest bath?"

"Gladiola did a fantabulous job. She displayed the candles and bath goodies Mom sent quite satisfactorily. I sent Mom a text letting her know the package arrived. I also reminded her that I don't need any more things for the house."

"Speaking of houses, I should get back to mine.

I'm finally making headway on my latest project. I've got lots of photos to sort through for my next coffee-table book. Too long of a break throws me off my game." Maggie snatched up stray pieces of bubble wrap and straightened the throw pillows, then fawned over the two Moses-style bassinets with leather handles, the woven exterior lined with lofty sheepskin, the wooden stands—everything Montana.

Maggie was the kind of mother I wanted my mother to be. The kind of mother I wanted to be for my children.

The phone rang, and Dad appeared in the kitchen doorway, looking like the rugged rancher he was.

"I'll answer the call," Maggie said.

"Hi, Dad."

He nodded and took off his hat. "I'll be glad when things settle down for you."

"Me too. Thanks for helping the guys with the furniture."

"You're welcome. We didn't lose too much of the day. Tristan and Justin are mending the fence, and Silas is tinkering with the tractor motor with Quinn."

I followed my father into the living room. He perched himself on the three-legged stool next to the hearth, and I stood in the archway with one ear to Maggie's conversation in the kitchen.

"That rug is a bit much. With enough spit-up, it might not last long." The dimple in his cheek appeared. "This stool reminds me of a dog I once had. He was a good pup." He held up three fingers.

"Seriously, you had a three-legged dog?"

The back door shut, and Maggie said hello to Matt. I peeked around the corner. Maggie had given him the phone. I looked back to Dad after I heard Matt end the call. He and Maggie's whispers were too hushed to discern.

"Yep. Paco. I'm not sure he even realized he was missing a leg." Dad scratched his whiskers. "You would've loved him. Paco was a cyclone when he chased his tail—kind of like someone else in this room." Dad's lip curled.

"You know me. I'm a sucker for an animal in need." I patted his shoulder. "And subtle, Dad. I hear you."

"Which reminds me. I received a call about a pinto named Sway." His brow curved with question.

"He needed a home, and he's healthy. Doc Neely checked him out. Next time, I'll discuss taking on another animal with you first. I promise."

"I've heard that before." Dad put his hat on and tugged at the brim. "Taking in strays has become an expensive habit."

"They're not exactly strays. It's not like I find them on the roadside."

"Close enough. There isn't a shelter or rancher who doesn't know your name when they're looking to unload an animal."

"You're exaggerating, and there are plenty of animals I haven't adopted."

Maggie joined us. She and Dad belonged together like salt and pepper or peanut butter and huckleberry jam.

Matt sauntered in, rubbing his chin. "I'm not sure what just happened."

"Who was on the phone? Is something wrong?" The hair on my nape prickled.

Matt nudged his white cowboy hat back. I noted the suspicious exchange between him and Maggie. He sat on the sofa and patted the seat beside him. "I have a surprise for you," he said.

I braced myself for a crash landing and then sat. "Do you know the sex of the babies? If you do, don't tell me. I want to be surprised. You know I told Dr.—"

"Hold on before you get yourself all riled up. I don't know the sex of the babies."

Matt's brown gaze melted my insides. Hopefully, our children would inherit his gentle disposition.

"Your mom phoned earlier. You were at the main house with Glad, and I intercepted the call. I told your mom you'd be here this afternoon to interview a nanny if she wanted to call back. She wanted me to tell you, she's cleared her calendar."

"You spoke to my mother earlier? What do you mean, *cleared her calendar?*"

"She's staying for eight weeks, starting tomorrow. Surprise."

My heart skipped a beat, the flash in my cheeks a scorcher. My body went limp against the leather cushions. No words came. Lola ran in, circled the living room, stopped long enough to bark at the faux bear rug, then laid down nose to nose with the shaggy beast.

Glad appeared in the doorway with a hot pickle and beef sandwich. "Did you tell her yet?"

"I couldn't get a word in edgewise. Your mom kept talking about the babies and meeting me and how much we'll need help since we're starting the interview process over again, and then I heard myself agree." Matt shoulders fell forward. "I didn't know what to do."

"Eight weeks?" I rested my elbow on the arm

of the sofa and cradled my forehead in the palm of my hand.

"Yay." Maggie clapped, her effort nothing less than sarcastic.

"You're not helping." Dad took her hand. "Come on, Glad. Chloe and Matt need some alone time. I'm not sure that sandwich will be much of a peace offering."

I gestured for Glad to leave the sandwich. Matt helped me to my feet. I touched each one of the seven silver horseshoes nailed to the mantel. "I have to interview the woman who's coming before dinner."

"That was her on the phone. She canceled. Sorry, babe. Will you be okay?" Matt's voice was quieter than usual.

I turned on a heel.

"What are you doing?" he asked.

"I'm going upstairs to find bigger pants."

SHADOWS DRIFTED ACROSS the ceiling as moonlight streamed in on the sandman's back. Although my eyelids were heavy, I doubted I'd sleep with my mother's gift of an eight-week stay weighing on my mind. She'd taken advantage of Matt and she wasn't even here yet.

I jammed a pillow between my legs, trying to get comfortable. Matt stepped through the doorway with a tray of food, his shadow tall and lean. He wore blue-striped sleeping pants with a hole in the knee and heavy socks. That was like him not to throw anything away, including me.

"You didn't join us for dinner. You must be starving. I brought you the sandwich Glad left."

"I doubt that'll make the nervous knots in my belly go away. Mom's taking this visit so seriously." The night sky shone through the skylight. The twinkly stars reminded me there would always be light. I closed my eyes and made a wish.

"Worrying isn't going to solve anything." Matt sat on the edge of the bed, handsome as ever.

I kicked off the blanket. "I suppose you think being all hunky is the perfect distraction. Won't the guys miss you?"

"The bunkhouse will do fine without me. Besides, I thought I should be here. It's your first night in a new place, and the babies might come." He handed me a leatherbound book from the tray. "Silas sends his best. He thought some poetry might clear your head."

"I'll have to thank him."

Silas hired on last fall and could sing a herd of cattle or horses into submission with his soothing serenades. He was burly, had a thick red beard, loved literature, could fix an engine, and was sweet as huckleberry pie.

"About your mother, she left me speechless. I didn't know what to say." Matt ran his fingers through his thick, dark hair.

"Initiations are tough." I fluffed the pillow between my legs. "I hadn't prepared myself for a surprise entrance. Rookie mistake."

"You'll feel better if you eat." He set the serving tray on the nightstand.

I resisted blaming my brooding behavior on raging hormones and the full moon. I'd wanted my mother to be here, and I'd gotten what I wanted.

"Thanks for staying with me, cowboy." The hem of my shirt inched up, and Matt kissed my belly. He didn't fight fair. He'd brought me my favorite sandwich, came to bed bare-chested, and his butterfly kisses sent a shiver down my spine.

"Can you blame her for wanting to be here? This is an exciting time. You should've heard her. She said the gift of time was perfect. She was so proud of herself for rearranging her schedule."

"She could sell lipstick to a monkey. You know this gift is nonexchangeable. And I was good with a *regular* visit. Eight weeks is more over the top than that rug lying on the living room floor. A lot can go wrong in eight weeks."

"Or a lot could go right." He took a bite of the sandwich then wiped his chin with the napkin.

The corner of my mouth lifted. "Just goes to show you, it's not possible to anticipate everything. Raising children is going to be the same. You know that, don't you?" I covered my face with a pillow, sighed, then stuffed it beneath bent knees.

"This sandwich sure is good." He took another slow, savory bite.

"You're nothing but trouble, cowboy." I held his face in my hands. The aroma of vinegar-soaked cukes and warm beef drew me in. "I'll have some of that sandwich before you eat the whole thing."

We took turns taking bites until it was gone. Matt set the food tray with the empty plate near the door. When he came back to bed, he ran his fingers across my collarbone and down to my belly.

"Thanks for taking the calves back to the pasture today. I wouldn't want them to wander too far or worse."

"I know, and you're welcome." Matt yawned. "They're lucky to have you. We all are."

"I feel the same way about you. Thanks for riding my Gypsy while I'm out of commission."

"I haven't been. She's been funny around me and not in a friendly way."

I propped myself up and stared at his profile. "What?"

"Getting between you and Gypsy is like tangoing with a rattlesnake. Although the music is mesmerizing, the—"

I touched his lips. "You probably shouldn't finish that thought. Acting funny, how?"

A glint of uncertainty flashed in Matt's eyes. He fidgeted with the seam at the shoulder of my T-shirt. "Ever since you stopped riding, I feel like she's got it *in* for me. Every time I get near her, she's nervous. Her ears twitch. I swear she tries to kick me when I'm not looking."

"You're imagining things."

"I'm not *imagining* anything. I'm staying clear of her."

"Come on, you're yanking my chain."

"No, I'm not." Matt lowered his gaze.

"You're a great rider. You can handle her."

"Sorry, Chloe. It's best if Gypsy and I remain distantly cordial for now. She's presently not a Matt Cooper fan, and I'd like to remain intact."

"You're serious." I shook my head in disbelief.

"She means business. She bucked me off last week."

"No, she didn't."

"Yes, she did. Justin's got the video on his phone."

"I'd like to see that."

"I bet you would." Matt gave me a sideways glance.

"I can't believe she's being a pill."

"I can. She *is* your horse."

"Is she hinky around Silas?"

"Yep. And he's got the critters in his back pocket like you do. His singing only spurs her on. Tristan's up for the challenge though."

"Always is. I'll talk to him." I rested my head on Matt's chest. His heart beat strong like the hooves of the herd at sunrise. "My mom's coming tomorrow."

"I know. It's time."

"She won't stay for eight weeks. She'll be homesick for Cali and her busy schedule, and the babies will overwhelm her. She's just being impulsive."

"Remember the good times, Chloe."

"I do, Matt. Can you hand me the purple journal in that nightstand drawer next to you, please?"

Matt took the tattered journal from the drawer and inspected it. "The lock is busted. This thing looks like it's been through a war."

"Childhood—close enough." I flipped through the pages of photos. "I see your smirk. Yes, I'm very entertaining. But seriously, things were way better when Dad and I moved to the ranch. I jimmied the latch so I wouldn't get locked out and forget her when we were apart." I ran my fingers across a faded color advertisement for perfume and sniffed the insert. "I love this scent. This is my mother. A floral bouquet layered with a warm woody base, vanilla and patchouli." I smiled and showed him the sealed plastic baggie in the back of the book with unopened scented inserts. "When I think she's *really* gone, the pictures I've taped in this book and her perfume bring her back."

"You miss her more than you let on."

"I do." I closed my journal and tucked it beneath my pillow for carefree dreaming.

CHAPTER 4

GYPSY AND I stood together at the pasture fence, taking in the landscape. The perfect sky reflected in the pond's glossy shimmer. "You've got to shape up. When Dr. Hennessey gives me the go-ahead, we'll ride up to the ridge. Grandpa's rosebush will need tending to." I stroked her cheek, thinking about the stone cross marking the spot where we'd scattered his ashes. "Maggie's working on her book, and my mother will be here soon. You should see the club chairs that were delivered this morning."

Gypsy nudged me with her velvety snout. Her whiskers tickled my skin. "I know. Two babies. I kind of blame Matt, too. But that's no reason to buck him off. You're gonna have to move on. Believe me. I know the struggle. Being a momma is going to be hard work. Do you think I could put a baby in each of your saddlebags?" I took in her affectionate gaze the color of rich cocoa. "I didn't think so."

She whipped her tail back and forth, then

whinnied. I rested my arms on the split rail fence and put my head down.

"What's eating you?"

I looked over my shoulder at Tristan. Even with my wide-brimmed cowboy hat pulled low, the sunlight blinded me, kind of like the news of having twins or Mom's impromptu decision to stay eight weeks. The past was bound to come up.

"Hey, Tristan. Aren't you supposed to be out with the cattle?"

"Yeah, I'll be heading back out in a few. We've got some feisty bulls today. You know I love a good challenge. I know you do, too."

"I'd give anything to be out there with you guys." I stroked Gypsy's dark hide and remembered a time when I told her that the star on her forehead was a gift from heaven.

"You will be soon enough." Tristan bumped his hat back. His crooked smile was reassuring.

"I'm glad you didn't turn out to be the jerk I thought you'd be," I said.

"Gee, thanks—I think." He tucked his leather gloves in his back pocket. "What a sincere compliment. Sarcastic as ever."

Gypsy snorted.

"Seriously, what's got you looking so nervous, bosslady?"

"My mom's coming today. It's been a long time, and I want everything to go smoothly."

Tristan had rustled my nerves with just his presence when he first got here. We'd had our scuffles and learned how to feed from each other's stubborn natures and inflated egos. Tristan could be hard around the edges, but losing his wife, Vivian, and son, James, in a car accident had devastated him. He missed them as much as I missed my granddad, and the caring cowboy emerging from the depths of grief made the sunshine brighter. I couldn't imagine the 617 Ranch without Tristan Donoghue. He had signed on with us almost a year ago, and we needed him as much as he needed us. I'd become attached to him as much as I had to his jokester brother, Justin, who seemed more like a brother to me than a hired hand.

"Seems like you should be more excited to see your mom," Tristan said.

"I'm not sure we've ever spent eight weeks together. That's 56 days, 1,344 hours. Guess the excitement is buried beneath the nerves." Gypsy nudged me again. I lost my balance. Tristan caught me and pushed me upright.

"Whoa there. We don't need you falling down."

"Gypsy sure will be happy when I can ride her again. That day won't get here soon enough."

"I'd sure like to have you out there, too," Tristan said.

"Really?" I fingered Gypsy's black mane.

"We spent too much time butting heads and racing to the front of the herd, trying to prove ourselves. We should've realized sooner we were on the same team." He paused. "It's been kind of lonely without your sass and competition out there. You're the best foreman I've worked for. But don't tell the guys I told you."

"Sure thing. And thanks," I said.

Reuniting with my mom shouldn't be much different from riding with the men. Being foreman meant sitting tall and creating unity among the crew. There was no place for doubt. I'd remember that if things got rocky, although vying for her attention shouldn't interfere now that she'd put work on the back burner.

"You're welcome. And by the way, that's how to deliver a compliment. No sarcasm needed," he said with a click of his tongue. "If there's anything I can do to help, let me know."

"If you see me running from the house, offer me a ride. Just kidding." I pointed to the sports car coming down the drive. "And that would be my mother."

"That's a mighty cloud of dust in her trail."

"And when it settles, you might find yourself with an outrageous faux bearskin rug or a pair of turquoise leather club chairs trimmed with exotic wood and brass studs. My house is starting to look like a showroom."

Tristan draped his arm around my shoulders and gave me a squeeze.

"Pretend your momma is one of those horses of yours. With a little sugar and gentle persuasion, you could make a beautiful connection," he said.

"Um, what's all the attention for?" I wrinkled my nose at him.

"I was told I had to be nice to you."

"Just when I thought you'd decided to be a decent human being." I swatted him, and he rolled his shoulders forward with a snort. "Apparently, you're more like Justin than I thought."

"Thank you," he said with a comical bow. He pulled his leather gloves from his back pocket and put them on. "I see you thinking about riding away. You best not entertain that thought if you know what's good for you. You jostle those babies around, and they'll be here sooner than you think."

"Like I could even get my leg over the back of the saddle."

"Viv was as thin as a rail when she was pregnant with James. Your personalities are similar. Determined. Independent. Resilient. One thing I learned from her was to never underestimate a woman." His voice was deep and tender.

"I would've liked her."

"Yes, you would've."

No one had told Tristan to be nice to me. No one told him to do anything. He relied on instincts and was finally letting his lighter side shine. The temperament of his compassion was influenced by kindheartedness.

"You stay off that horse. Gypsy will understand." He pointed a serious finger at me and lowered his chin.

"Will you take Gypsy for a ride?"

"You want me to do what?" He planted his hands on his hips.

"You heard me. She'd love the run."

"You sure?"

"I wouldn't have asked if I didn't mean it," I said. "She's bucked Matt from the saddle, but you probably already know that."

"What's in it for me?"

"The pure satisfaction of knowing you're the only one who can talk to her like I do. How'd you put it?" I cleared my throat and grunted. "I bet with a little sugar and gentle persuasion, you could make a beautiful connection."

"Gypsy ain't no woman." Tristan hooked his thumbs in his belt loops.

"Sounds like you've been hanging around Trout." Gypsy rested her chin on my shoulder, her breath like soft whispers in my ear. "You best be careful. She knows what you're saying. And for the record, the sisterhood doesn't favor ribs like that."

Tristan kicked at the dirt.

"Will you do it, cowboy?"

"Do I have to sign a waiver, bosslady?"

"No waivers. You'd be doing me and Gypsy a huge favor."

"I'll ride her under one condition." His gaze brightened.

"Lay it on me."

"You agree to an old-fashioned horse race when you're cleared to ride."

"Are you kidding me? I'm all in. It'll give me something to look forward to."

Gypsy shook her head, then ran into the pasture. She laid in her favorite spot, her hooves slashing the air as she rolled in the grass.

"Figured so. Besides, by the time you're ready, Casanova will be up for the challenge. He's turning into a stellar ride."

"Seems to me, your friend Branch has found himself a pushover when it comes to unloading a difficult horse."

"I haven't taken them all." Tristan scratched his chin. "Seems to me, you're quite the sucker for a homeless animal, too."

"Yeah, totally. Do you ever think they know they're not wanted or the real reason someone they love can't keep them?" I stared at my mom through the windshield of her car as she rummaged through her purse for who knew what: her favorite lipstick, a business card from someone she met in an LA airport bar, my childhood.

"I think so." Tristan whistled, and Gypsy got on all fours and ran to the fence. "She and I have been discussing this race for a bit now. She's on Team Tristan."

"You wish, Donoghue. We're gonna smoke ya."

Mom got out of her car and waved. She pulled the cell phone away from her ear and shook it. Tristan patted Gypsy's twitching wither. A sure sign she needed to run.

"I know, girl. All in due time." I tickled her nose until she sneezed.

"Woohoo! We've got ourselves a race," Tristan whooped.

"Tristan's gone a little kooky, hasn't he?" I shooed Gypsy away, and she ran across the pasture, kicking up her heels along the way.

"And good luck to you, too." He skipped off, whistling an upbeat tune.

Like Tristan said, hopefully, a little sugar would sweeten the pot with my mother. "Hi, Mom. You look great." I played with the hem of my cotton tunic, the blue embroidery like miniature mountains beneath my fingertips.

"What's wrong with my phone?" She leaned against the cherry red convertible.

"It's not your phone. Reception is spotty out here."

"Oh, that's right. All those dropped calls we've suffered in the middle of great debates, and the communication void after your last visit. We've got eight weeks, daughter—this'll be the reunion we deserve." Her all-knowing smile appeared forgiving. "Hey, did those club chairs come? I know you told me you didn't need anything else, but your message came after I bought them. Very Western. Very Montana elegant."

"I put them in my office. Thank you." A cool breeze kissed my collarbone. "Park closer to the old house, and I'll find someone to help us with your bags."

Mom peered over the rim of her designer sunglasses. "I'm looking forward to staying with you and Matt."

"Matt's bunking with the guys. You and I will have the place to ourselves." I left out the part about him not moving in until I was ready. I'd save that tidbit for later, much later.

She poked her cell phone screen. "Was that Matt I saw making you laugh?"

"Nope. Hired hand. Animal whisperer." I wasn't sure how to interpret the pout on Mom's face. Her lips appeared fuller than the last time I saw her. She didn't need touch-ups. "I'll meet you at the house. I see the car rental found you a sporty, suitable ride."

"They most certainly did." Mom rested her hand on the hood and struck one of her famous poses. She'd reinvented herself from a top model into a fashion guru, mentor to aspiring models, and consultant to continue what she did best: pose for the camera and live her best life in the Hollywood limelight.

"I wouldn't worry about the phone. We have a landline if you need it."

"What do you mean *if* I need it? I'll need a phone. I'll be working with Hermione long-distance. We've got several meetings scheduled to discuss marketing."

I digested her definition of *clearing a calendar*. I'd have to snap off another leg from one of the many broken trophies I'd squirreled away when no one was looking. My mother was a workaholic.

"Sorry, Mom, I can't fix the phone situation. That's why we carry two-way radios when we ride or go out. Try using your phone in the house." I waited for her scowl to soften. "I'll meet you there."

"You don't want a ride?"

I touched the hood of the car, the glossy sheen warm. "The only ride I want is from that dark, four-legged beauty with the sleek mane. Besides, I'd rather walk. If I sit in that car, I might not be able to get out." I rested my hand on my stomach and drummed my fingers. I didn't care what kind of car she drove. The luxury vehicle gene was not part of my DNA. Grandpa's vintage pickup truck suited me fine. That little voice inside my head urged caution and to keep my chin up.

The engine of Mom's car hummed. A familiar cool breeze lifted my spirits. An image of my grandmother, Ida May, interrupted my thoughts, her face framed by Grandpa's truck window, her hair pulled back, her eyes fixed on the horizon like she was watching my grandpa work his magic with the cattle and horses.

Tiny yellow flowers the color of butter dotted the grass lining the rocky path home. Stalks of thistle reminded me of life's prickly moments, and I looked forward to the midsummer purple blooms I loved.

My mother drove past, beeping the horn.

I rubbed my belly and talked to the twins like I did when I thought of important life details. "If I could, I'd run alongside the car, making my own trail of dust. I'd chase my momma and hug her so hard, she'd squeal. Something for you to think about. No one will love you like I do."

CHAPTER 5

NEWS TRAVELED FAST. Trout waited on the deck for Mom and me.

"Thanks for helping with the luggage." I eyed the path leading to Trout's cabin. "I'm still not running," I said.

"You made that clear."

"Where's Matt?"

"In the north field with your daddy and the others."

"What about Maggie and Glad?"

"You can keep asking, but they're not coming. You're stuck with me. Call me a softy, but I didn't think you should be left in the chute alone. Those broncos come down mighty heavy."

"Thanks, Trout. But Mom and I will be fine. She's not wearing her spurs."

"You're welcome. I'll stay long enough to carry in the bags and make sure you've cleared the gate."

"By the way, nice job with the rodeo analogy."

"Again, you're welcome. But I'm not waiting for your nod. If I did, I'd be here all day, and this old guy has a fishing pole rigged and ready to go."

"You're hardly old." I stared at him. His care-worn skin and swagger defined the word *timeless*.

"From my vantage point, I beg to differ." Trout hooked his thumbs in his front pockets.

"Remind me of your age," I said.

"Nice try, kid. We ain't talking about age."

Mom parked her car beneath a shade tree in the yard and popped the trunk.

"That's your cue, cowboy."

Mom got out and joined me on the deck. Trout heaped her luggage on the lawn. By the strain in his jaw and the three trips he took in and out of the house, she hadn't packed light.

"It's good to see you, Mom."

"I don't think I gave you a proper hello back there." She took my hands in hers, stepped back, and inspected me from head to toe. "It's good to see you, too."

"How was your flight?"

"The flight was on time. The pilot was handsome. He gave me his number." She leaned closer. "I'm looking forward to meeting Matt. It's funny how I've never met him before."

"The universe works in mysterious ways," I said.

"Yes, it is amusing how the Chloe universe

works." She drew me in and hugged me. "I'm so glad we're doing this."

"Me too. I want you to know the babies. I want us to get back on track."

"Mothers and daughters are supposed to make up for lost time during monumental milestones. We have so much to catch up on."

We had more than a little lost time to account for. We had *a lot* of catching up to do. There were things I wanted to know. I had questions about chunks of time in her life she didn't talk about. It was time to understand her need to put work before relationships.

Trout fiddled with the squeaky screen door handle before coming out of the house.

"Welcome back to the ranch. It's been a while," he said.

"Like—twenty years. Give or take a year or two." Mom drew her sunglasses down to the end of her nose and peered over the rim. "You haven't changed a bit."

His cheeks went rosy with the smile beneath his bushy, white moustache. "Your bags are in your room. Hope you enjoy your stay." He nodded and walked away whistling a cowboy tune.

"Come in." I gestured for Mom to follow me inside, held the mudroom door open, and showed her to the kitchen. "Want something to drink?"

"Would I ever. It's probably too early for a cocktail though."

"I'd say so. It's not even close to five o'clock. We've got water, soda, lemonade, and iced tea."

"Water would be nice." She patted her cheeks. "It's quite warm, and the airplane air dehydrates the skin."

"Has it really been that long?" I poured her a glass of sparkling water with a slice of lime, just the way she liked it.

"The last time I was here we had that crazy Christmas. Maggie's dog was lost, and we spent all that time looking for him. Bones was a stinker."

"And that man from the moving company looked like Santa. I was eight. It was my first Christmas here. I think Bones's return qualified as a Christmas miracle." I filled another glass with ice water and took a long draw. "We hung up all those fliers in Bozeman, and you bought me a fur hat. I loved that thing. You made me feel like a snow princess."

Mom made her way into the living room and dropped her oversized designer purse on the ottoman. "Wow, you've done some work in here."

"I keep forgetting you've been here before." I followed and wondered when she'd notice the bear rug's frightening stare.

"Me too. It's a bit surreal," she said, peeking through the open French doors to the sunroom I'd turned into my office. "Those chairs are exquisite. You'd have to be nuts not to like them." She caressed the supple turquoise leather. "You remembered how I like my water. Thank you. You've got a good start. Would you like me to help with the finishing touches? Maybe cow print chairs or pillows for the living room. I saw the quaintest antique stores on the drive here. How about an armoire for the empty corner?"

"I appreciate the offer, but no thanks."

"I knew you'd say that." She lowered her gaze.

"What did you buy at the antique store?" I crossed my arms and leaned against the doorjamb.

"A little something for your office. You've grown up, and it's exciting to see you working with your father. The light in this room is spectacular."

"It is, isn't it?" I lifted my chin to the sunlight streaming in. I could see the main house, and the view of the mountains was like a painting. "What did you buy?"

"A desk. I know you said you were set, and I promise this is the last thing."

"I hope so. I'd really like to make this place

mine." I waited for a reaction and got none. "The chairs bring out the turquoise blue in the Navajo rug. I approve."

"A lovely combination, I'd say. I've taken the liberty of doing some research regarding your nanny dilemma. I've found three candidates to take my place when I leave you in eight weeks."

Mom may have crossed the line when it came to extending her stay, but part of me was pleased she'd found someone to interview. I knew she'd exhaust the pool of candidates. She wanted the best for her grandchildren, and so did I. The sliver of common ground helped bridge the gap between us.

"Let's interview them right away. The sooner I get this locked down, the better. One of these women is right, I can feel it. No Boca Raton, no unreasonable schedules, no tagalongs, no *I'm allergic to horses*." I took in Mom's frown. "Mom"—I pointed to my belly—"they're coming any day. Maybe any minute. We need the help."

Mom cradled my face in her hands. "Slow down. There's no hurry. Let's work on finding you the *right* nanny, the *right* way. Take our time, hire an investigator if we need to."

"An investigator?"

"Gotcha. This is fun already."

I flashed her a toothy smile and changed lanes without a blinker. "I saw your feature in *La Chic*."

"And yes, a background check may warrant a private investigator." She drained her glass of water. "Did you read the article or just skim the photos? Aren't the clothes fabulous? Hermione and I have become good friends, but you already knew that. This collaboration has created a fashion splash bigger than we both imagined. I don't know how I could ever repay her for her support. Her guidance has gotten me through some tough times."

"Was I one of those *tough times*?"

"Yes, Chloe. You were." She took my hands in hers.

"I should've called sooner," I said.

"I'm here now, and that's all that matters."

"I did read the article. You never cease to amaze me." I regretted not being there for her. Standing up for myself may have been necessary, but cutting her off hadn't solved our issues or how I felt when her work overshadowed my presence. "I'm happy you have Hermione."

Mom left my office, gasped, then crouched to inspect the faux bear rug's menacing stare.

"Oh my. I guess the photo you sent wasn't a joke. Maybe we can have that altered. This rug may not have been the best choice after all."

"I agree. At some point, I'll find it a suitable home."

"I'm sure you will." She set her glass on the end table in the living room and opened the manilla envelope she pulled from her purse. "I want to show you the nanny bios I have. I've numbered them. Greatest potential is number one."

I skimmed the printed bios. "Um, Mom, I didn't sign up on the Rock-A-Bye Baby website. I've got the position listed with two other services. And I really do like your clothing line. You and Hermione make a good team. What's she like in the real world?"

"I know you didn't post here. I found your profile on Nursery Times and Pat-A-Cake." She pulled out a printed copy of my ad. "But I can't see who's responding, so I created another profile on another trending platform." She looked up. "I *am* your mother. And Hermione is persistent when it comes to achieving her goals. Her flare and style are impeccable. Her designs are more than fashion—they tell a story. She's down-to-earth and organic. You'd really like her."

"Not to be ungrateful, but you could've given me a head's up."

"I'm sorry. I didn't think making an account in your name would be a big deal. Would you like me to take it down?"

I reviewed the three profiles for the potential candidates. "Not yet. I may have overreacted. Imagine that." My gaze met my mother's. "And I'd like to get to know Hermione someday."

Mom didn't attempt to hide her grin.

"Great. I've already called references for Carol, number one, and Maria, number two. They both check out."

"Dang, you're efficient." I bit the inside of my cheek after the words slipped out.

Mom starred Maria's application. "This young lady's photo has great energy. She's worked in daycare. Has transportation. Likes animals. Is willing to start dinner for you, does laundry, diaper duty, light housework. Very nice references. Seems to possess common sense."

"I'm almost afraid to ask. Have you scheduled interviews?"

"I didn't go that far, dear. Give me some credit."

"Thanks, Mom. I appreciate that."

She turned on her phone, dialed the first reference for Ashley, candidate number three, and clicked on the speaker. "Do you want to ask the questions?"

"Yes." I sipped my water, then set the glass down.

On the third ring, someone answered, and that someone sounded like a young child.

"Hello. May I please speak with Helen?" I asked.

Mom and I waited for a response.

"Is someone there? Helen?" I tapped the phone. Had the call cut out?

"She can't talk right now."

"This is Chloe McIntyre. Could you please have Helen call me back? I can leave my number."

I skimmed Ashley's resumé. She'd worked in multiple childcare positions, had three children, noted cooking skills, and had background in early education. She'd also required two weeks' notice should there be any scheduling changes. With three children hanging on her coattails, how much notice would she give me when something went haywire at her end?

"Helen's sleeping. I can only get her up if it's a 'mergency. I'm not 'posed to turn on the stove or open the door."

"Okay, then. Can I ask you a question before I hang up?"

"I guess so."

"Do you know how to call someone if there is

an emergency?"

"I push 9-1-1. I'm six."

"That's good to—" The call ended.

Mom's phone rang almost immediately. She pointed to the number displayed on the screen and put the caller on speakerphone.

"Hello," I said.

"This is Helen. Did you call a minute ago?" She sounded irritated.

"Yes, I did. My name is Chloe McIntyre. Ashley's interested in the nanny position I have listed and noted you as a reference. Do you have a moment to chat?"

Helen yawned. "Oh, yeah. Ashley told me about this. She's real excited about taking care of babies and the hours. She can work from six to four and still have time to pick up a shift at the bar."

"Great. I appreciate your time. Have a good day," Mom said, then hung up before Helen could say anything else. "That won't work."

"Maybe not, but you could've at least let me finish the call."

"Sorry. And that's why I'm *efficient*."

"Let's divide and conquer. Are you positive there were no red flags with Maria's or Carol's references?"

"You can call if you'd like."

"Let's set up the interviews. I'll call if I have questions. Actually, if I have doubts after meeting them, I'll keep looking. I'll call Maria. You call Carol," I said.

"Sounds like you're pretty efficient yourself." Mom smiled. "This is our time, daughter."

I fanned away the hormones ruffling feelings I'd stowed deep inside.

Mom rolled her shoulders. Her jawline softened. "I know I haven't always been dependable. I want to change that."

"I know." The corner of my mouth lifted. "Let's get these calls done and enjoy the rest of the day."

I went into the kitchen to give my mother privacy. When Maria didn't pick up, I left a message, leaned against the counter, and rubbed the bridge of my nose. I needed to take a breath and relax. Mom had shown up on time, done nanny research, and even said the bear rug was too much. If Mom didn't buy any more furniture, we'd be fine.

Mom came in with her phone pressed to her ear and handed me a note that read *4:00, today?*

"Just a second, Carol," she said.

"The sooner, the better." I pointed to my baby belly.

Mom gave Carol the address and ended the call.

"I'm telling you. Finding a nanny is harder than you think. Carol will be number nine. I hope one of these ladies works out." I crossed my fingers.

FOUR O'CLOCK ROLLED around, and Carol—nanny candidate number one—hadn't shown. Mom and I sat in the Adirondack chairs on the deck, enjoying the late afternoon sun.

"We're doing well so far," Mom said. "Thanks for inviting me to the ranch."

"I'd say so. Thanks for coming to see me." I shaded my brow and glanced at her flawless profile. "How long do we wait for Carol? If she's late now, I'm wondering if she's late when she works. Has she called or texted?"

Mom shook her head. "Any response from Maria?"

I checked my phone. "Nope."

Mom perked up. "Maybe that's Carol in the red truck." She pointed toward the bridge. "Is that your father following in the pickup?"

I tried to get up but couldn't. "I should've known better than to sit in this chair."

Mom stood, grabbed my hands, and helped me stand.

"Wow, Mom. You're stronger than you look." I tugged the hem of my shirt over my exposed belly. "I hope it's Carol, and, yes, that's Dad."

"Pilates, weights, and Paulo. He's Brazilian and fabulous."

"That's too much information."

Carol parked her truck in the drive next to Granddad's vintage pickup. Mom and I watched on, eager to meet her.

"Paulo's my personal trainer, not a partner. Relax."

"What do you think of her so far?" I asked, trying not to move my lips.

"She looks like a Sunday school teacher."

Carol got out of the truck, waved, and made her way toward us.

"Hi, there. I'm Chloe McIntyre. This is my mom, Brook."

"You look like you'll be having those babies any day now. Such a glow. Your profile noted you're having twins. I'm Carol Dillard." She fanned her cheeks. "You'll have to excuse my chatter. I'm excited to meet you and a wee bit nervous."

My phone buzzed with a text from Dad.

Who's the woman?

Possible nanny, I replied.

Dad turned the truck around and drove away.

"Please. Come in. So, you were an elementary school music teacher?" I held the door for her.

"Yes. Thirty-one years." She straightened the collar of her blouse and grinned.

After a quick tour of the first floor, I showed her back to the kitchen to chat further.

"This is a gorgeous home," Carol said.

"Thank you. My grandparents built it. Should this be a good fit, I'd like you to come out before I go back to work full-time, to learn my routine and meet the people you'll be seeing around the ranch. Obviously, I'm looking for someone who can begin soon." My phone buzzed again. I read the screen and tried not to react. "Sorry about the interruption. It's my father."

"Well, maybe not start immediately. I'm staying for eight weeks," Mom said with a smile.

"Regardless of how long my mother stays, I'd like you to get acquainted with the place."

Standing next to Carol, I explained the list of duties and expectations. While she and Mom chatted about diapers and bottles, I leaned over and sniffed. Mom looked at me funny. Carol leaned away, and by the expression on her face, I'd been caught.

There was a knock at the back door.

"Mom, can you hold that thought for a minute?" I went into the mudroom. Dad held up two empty mini-bottles of vodka. "Are you sure?"

"I was behind her. She tossed these out the window before she pulled in the drive. She's got four more full ones in the console." Dad went into the kitchen.

I wasn't prepared for a showdown.

"Hi, Carol. I'm John McIntyre, Chloe's father. Nice to meet you." He took off his leather gloves and tucked them in his back pocket.

Carol greeted him with a cordial smile. I hadn't noticed the smudge of red lipstick on her teeth until now.

"You lost these back there on the road." He showed her the two empty vodka bottles. "I'd be glad to call a ride for you."

The color drained from her face. "I'll see myself out," she said.

Dad escorted Carol to her truck. She got in, started the engine, and drove away. Dad followed her, keeping a safe distance behind. Mom and I raised our brows at each other.

"Good thing I cleared my schedule. Eight weeks might not be long enough."

There was no waiver in my mother's intent to stay on. I swallowed the knot at the back of my throat, tucked my hands into my pockets, and crossed my fingers.

"Come on, Maria!" we both said in unison.

"Jinx. You owe me a soda." Our voices married, and we laughed.

"I'll have my soda in a wineglass," Mom said.

"I'll stick to ginger ale."

Mom's smile led me to believe we could grow from *our* rocky bottom into the light, where we could see each other for what we were—like Montana sunflowers, following the sun in synchronicity.

CHAPTER 6

S NUGGLED BENEATH MY downy blanket, I'd slept through the country tune I'd programmed to wake me. I never slept through the alarm. Getting up before sunrise had become habit when I'd moved here as a child. My inner clock rose and set with the sun.

I wiped away the sleep and swung my legs over the side of the bed.

Last night, Mom and I had stayed up talking by the fire. Me with my glass of warm milk, she with her flute of prosecco. We'd stuck to discussing a nanny, the herds, and her latest business adventure with Hermione. Shallow conversation provided an opportunity to get our bearings before venturing into the deeper parts of us, where the wake stirred doubt and the things we didn't understand about each other.

After a quick shower, I dressed and went downstairs. Mom sat at the kitchen table with a sketchbook and colored pencils. I peeked over her shoulder and watched her sketch blouses.

"What if you added fringe on the embroidered hem of that smoky blue top with the V-neck?" My suggestion earned me one of my mother's approving smiles. "Just because I don't like to shop doesn't mean I don't like clothes. I know what I want, and most of the time I can't find it. How come you didn't wake me?" I stirred the warm oatmeal I'd made for breakfast, topped it with a sliced banana, and filled a tumbler with orange juice.

"You needed to sleep. We both had a big day yesterday." She added wispy fringe to her sketch. "This is a great idea. Thanks. What color?"

"White."

"I'd choose white, too." She noted the color in the margin.

"Um, did you really show up and go straight into Mom mode, or was I dreaming? Did Carol exist?"

"Yes, I went into Mom mode. It's time I stepped up to the plate. I did a rather fine job." She lowered her gaze. "And yes, Carol existed. Any response from number two yet?" She stood and poured herself another cup of coffee.

"No. But I'm glad you investigated other nanny resources. I didn't realize finding someone would be so difficult." I inspected the nearly empty wine bottle. "Wow, this prosecco must've been from an exceptional harvest."

"Did I drink the whole thing?"

I tipped the bottle toward the light. "Almost."

"Must be the altitude."

"Must be." I studied my mom.

The pockets of her designer denim glistened with sparkly embellishments, way pricier than my plain jeans with the red tag sewn into the seam. I was sure she hadn't bought one of those infomercial contraptions supplied with enough sequins and rhinestones to clog the best of vacuum cleaners.

Mom's blonde hair cascaded over her shoulders in silky ribbons. The buttons on her plaid shirt gleamed like freshwater pearls. She was glitz and glam. I was the laid-back tune of Montana crickets. The tomboy in me didn't identify with the makeup and curling iron she'd said good morning to.

"Oh, come on, Chloe. I have a glass of wine most nights. I haven't seen you in ages. I was a ball of nervous excitement, wound up from traveling and meeting Matt."

"You didn't meet Matt. He drove Lola to the vet after getting cleaned up. She's got an eye infection. He didn't get back until late. Remember?" Mom had wine at dinner, too. Her more-than-edgy response and inaccurate recall put me on edge, though I did my best to mute my usual impulse to make a hasty conclusion. "Any more leads on your end?"

"No," she replied.

"Did you sleep okay, Mom?"

"Surprisingly, I did."

"You'd better be careful." My caution pertained to more than sleeping well. "The fresh air will sneak up on you, not to mention the wine, and you won't want to leave." The words came out sweeter than a handful of honeysuckle.

She rinsed off a bunch of red grapes, set them on the table next to the plate of muffins, then touched my cheek. We sat across from each other. I imagined my dad sitting with his mom as a young boy at this very table, eating a hearty plate of pancakes and talking about horses, cattle, and school.

How come it took us so long to get here? Should I trust her with my heart? Why couldn't she understand I craved her presence, not her lifestyle? The one-upping and desire to outdo shadowed the simple things within reach.

"I can make you eggs and bacon if you like," I said. "Not very well, but I could give it a shot."

"Fruit and a muffin is more than enough." She

pushed the crumbs into a neat pile.

"I forgot, you're watching your weight." I rubbed my belly. From my point of view, I was more bloated than a bag of marshmallows.

"It's a lifestyle, Chloe." Mom set the butter knife down.

Was the absurd amount of wine a lifestyle, too? Or was she really that nervous about being here? "The altitude can make you ravenous. Try this. You need to eat more." I scooted the jar of huckleberry jam toward her. She unscrewed the lid, sniffed it, then read the label. "Paulo can fix you when you get home. A little bit won't matter," I said.

"Living in Montana can be mighty dangerous." She dipped a spoon into the jam, then savored the dollop until the spoon was licked clean.

"Bears and mountain lions could pose a problem if you're unlucky enough to cross paths."

"I meant the handsome wranglers, sweet air, hypnotizing landscape, and an appetite that craves all the above. There's certainly a draw." She rested her chin in the palm of her hand; her aquamarine gaze sparkled.

"I wouldn't live anywhere else." I drank my juice. My belly rolled over with two babies doing the backstroke. "Besides, it's not like I ever had a chance to live with you." I played with the hem of the placemat, regretting my choice of words. "I don't know where that came from." I ran my finger around the rim of my empty glass. "We both know that's a lie. I just wish you would've given it a try."

Hurt seeped past her long lashes.

"I'm going to have to learn how to get your attention without the stinging jabs. I'm sorry, Mom." The babies kicked, and I grabbed my sides.

"Are you okay, Chloe?"

"I think so." I took a deep breath and waited for another jolt. "Guess they're trying to tell me I don't have to say everything that pops into my head."

"No, you don't. I'm aware of my shortcomings. I can't change the past."

She held my hand. I'd forgotten how much I missed her touch.

"I want to be here for you, Chloe. Maybe you're not ready for this visit."

I finished my oatmeal and laid the spoon in the empty bowl the color of Italian vanilla gelato. Neither one of us spoke until she finished her coffee and collected her colored pencils.

"Maggie and your dad seem very happy," she said.

Guilt slithered through me. Maggie felt like home, and my mother knew it.

Sadness drifted into her eyes. If she'd had a long-term relationship, she kept it to herself. I doubted she had time to be part of a couple. I plucked grapes and popped them in my mouth before I could ask. She was a one-woman show. I knew about being a one-woman show, too, and I wanted her to know that she didn't have to be. I was here for her.

"They are," I said, the tug in my heart very real.

"And you and Matt? Are you happy?"

"Yes." Heat singed my cheeks. Talking about my personal life wasn't something I was good at.

"Be sure you are before moving in together or saying I do to Matt or anyone else."

"Marriage is off the table," I blurted out.

"Maybe right now it is, but people and feelings have a way of changing. You're moving in that direction, aren't you?"

"Matt and I are happy."

"Well"—she checked the time on her phone—"you've always known what you wanted."

"Kind of like someone else sitting at this table. Are you disappointed with me, Mom?"

"How can I be disappointed? I'm not even sure

I know you anymore." She swished her coffee around in the cup.

I drummed my fingertips on the table.

"Come on, Chloe. You've haven't made it easy. Neither of us have."

"Getting your attention is tough."

"You've got it now. For eight weeks. And I wasn't thinking about being disappointed. I was thinking you're more together than I ever was at your age. You know what you want and know how to get it. You know what you're willing to put up with or *not* to put up with. I should've sought out a therapist a long time ago." She sighed. "The high of my relationship with your dad took us down roads we never thought we'd go. The voids we were trying to fill had nothing to do with each other. Or you." She clutched the cup between her hands.

"You have a therapist?"

"Yes. I started seeing Dr. Clifton after our last visit."

"Dad took me to a therapist in elementary school when I struggled with not having you around. He called her the talking doctor. I liked her, and she made me feel better." I put the lid on the jam, then took my daily vitamin. "What was your void with Dad? I want to understand. I want not to say hurtful things. I want us to be close."

She set her cup on the table and fiddled with the handle. "Your dad's attention made me feel like somebody. Made me feel important. People consulted him. He knew how to help and heal them."

"You were somebody. Still are. You own the camera, for Pete's sake. People buy magazines, clothes, and product because of you." I rested my elbows on the table.

"Yes, but your father was *real*. Even with all the media attention, I was extremely lonely. Connecting with a camera doesn't humanize a person's needs." Mom tucked her hair behind her ears and lowered her lashes. "Then when I found out I was pregnant, I was afraid."

"Afraid of what?"

"Afraid I'd lose myself even more. Afraid I'd get stuck in suburbia and be expected to join a mother's club. Afraid I'd screw you up, make your life even harder."

"So you left me with Dad." I folded my hands.

"Leaving you with your father was best. He was more equipped to take care of you." Her sigh was deeper and bigger than the last one. "I've never said that before."

I picked at the hangnail on my thumb, the sting

a temporary diversion from the honesty. "When we talked about keeping this visit on an even keel, it seemed like it would be easier than it is. I'm not sure I can do this without bringing up my own issues. The last thing I want is to make you feel bad."

"I won't have my daughter second-guessing herself." Mom smoothed out the linen napkin she'd folded. "I'd like to give *us* a chance."

I braced the arms of my chair and pushed myself up. Mom cleared the table, and I excused myself. The horseshoe hanging above the doorway fell to the ground with a thud. I bent down to pick it up but couldn't reach around my belly. Wetness pooled at the corners of my eyes. I left the omen on the floor and went outside.

Calves 311 and 313 grazed in the yard. "I'm glad you're here. You must've known I needed you." Number 311 nudged my belly; 313 sniffed the grass near my feet, her ear tickling the back of my hand. I fed them treats from my pocket and eyed the path to Trout's cabin.

"I need you, too," I said to the babies. "Remember that when we don't see eye to eye. I'm pretty sure I'm gonna make mistakes."

The back door clapped shut. Mom walked across the deck to the stairs. Taking a deep breath, she tucked her hands in the back pockets of her jeans.

"If this is too much right now, I'll leave. The choice is yours. Just say the word. Like I said, it's your call, and I'll say that I understand even if I don't. I've got my therapist on speed dial." The tiniest of smiles crept into the seam of her lips.

I scratched 313's head while 311 sought out a patch of sweetgrass. Then 313 nudged me closer to the deck with her black nose.

"I'm here because of you, Chloe."

Hair bristled on the back of my neck. Ida May wouldn't have ignored me when I was a child. She would have raised me, afraid or not.

I imagined myself sitting beside her in Grandpa's vintage pickup truck bumping along the gravel road to the ranch after a long drive into town for groceries, Voodoo, my stuffed purple cat, along for the ride. Grandma would've been strict and warranted proper manners. She would've loved me like Maggie did.

If I wanted a relationship with my mother, I had to stop comparing the women in my life. Mom met me at the bottom of the deck stairs and rested her hand on my shoulder.

"If I would've stayed, your dad would've been more miserable, and you, too. It wouldn't have been good for any of us."

I glanced back at her. Her stare was inviting.

"And you wouldn't have Maggie," she added. "As much as I hate to admit it, things worked out for the best."

Calf 313 rested her nose on my belly. Her gaze was fixed on me as if she were reading my mind. Calf 311 headed toward the river. "Stay out of the water," I scolded. Calf 311 batted her eyelashes and replied with a sweet snort.

"Sounds like you're a mother already, Chloe."

"Hardly," I replied. "Seriously, Matt had to go in and get her. He was *not* happy." My voice trembled.

"But he did, right?"

"Yes, he did."

"Sounds like he's ready to be a father, too. I can't wait to meet him at dinner. I have a confession."

"Just one?" I joked.

"For now." Mom stroked 313's hide, her stance softened. "There's not a day I don't think about you. My life has snowballed into everything I ever wanted. But there's a part of me that wants so much more. Dr. Clifton suggested I do something about it. When Hermione and I designed the collection in the magazine, I couldn't get enough of her roots. Learning about her Crow heritage inspired me and strengthened our friendship and my understanding of so many things. Like you— she knows about cattle, horses, nature, and the land. I saw an opportunity."

"You always see opportunity."

"That's not a bad thing, Chloe. Let me finish." The curve of her lips fell flat.

Mom straightened her long tresses, made a ponytail, and wrapped it in a loose bun on the crown of her head, where I imagined she propped her tiara when attending one of her extravagant galas.

"I'm listening." I tucked my hands into my back pockets.

"When you called to tell me you were pregnant, I saw an opportunity to get to know you in a way I've not had the chance to. These babies are a fresh start, a chance to grow together, not further apart. I know I can't change the past. My recent designs didn't come from some harebrained idea— they were my way of getting you into my life again. They're a connection, they represent your essence, the essence I know to be true despite our difficulties."

"Is the therapist helping you with the wine habit? Are you an alcoholic?" My mother didn't need another struggle. And *we* didn't need another wedge to come between us.

"No, Chloe. I'm not, and I don't want to be. Stepping away from my Cali life for a hot second doesn't mean that stress isn't still present. I forgot about this place. The feelings. Coming here isn't a vacation or just getting to know the babies or apologizing for misguided behavior. Coming here has opened a past I thought I'd never revisit. The wine takes the edge off. In my mind, it's like liquid courage."

"You don't need liquid courage. What are you afraid of?"

"Losing you forever."

"I don't want you to lose me either." I focused on the distant mountaintops flecked with snow. Mom wrapped her arm around my shoulder. I melted into her, and she let me. We'd have to walk the fine line between the past and the present, and her delicate perfume blanketed me in hope.

CHAPTER 7

TRISTAN CAME UP the gravel drive, riding Gypsy. I shaded my eyes, assessed the grimace on his face, and called to him, "You looking for these two?"

"You're harboring fugitives, ma'am." Tristan dismounted Gypsy, then tied her to the hitching post beneath the shade tree and tipped his hat to Mom with a nod.

"I hardly think of my cattle friends as fugitives," I said.

"We keep fixing the fencing, and they keep finding new ways out. Can't seem to keep tabs on them, but we know where to find them. They sure do have a liking for you."

"What can I say? It's all part of my charm." I patted my Gypsy's neck. "Hi, girl. Tristan hasn't wasted any time getting you out here."

"If I'm gonna win our race fair and square, this girl needs exercise," he said.

"Hi, I'm Chloe's mom, Brook."

"Nice to meet you, ma'am."

Mom frowned. The last thing she wanted was to be called ma'am, and I couldn't wait for someone to call her grandma.

"She's just Brook. You can skip the ma'am. Reminds her of grannies, antique spectacles, and frilly blouses buttoned to a stern chin."

"What race? You can't ride in your condition, Chloe."

"Not now, Mom. After the babies come and the doctor says it's okay. I'm pretty good at it." By the look on Mom's face, she realized she hadn't seen me on a horse since I was a young girl.

Tristan knocked his hat back. "I'll say. She can whop just about anyone when she's rounding up strays or running free."

"Um, I can whop y'all," I said with a snap of my fingers.

Mom crossed her arms over her chest and inspected me from head to toe.

"It's true, Mom. Trout will tell you. I'm the bee's knees."

"Of course he will. He'd give his right arm for you. But that's neither here nor there. I'd like to see you ride." She stroked 311's back. The tension in her brow disappeared. "These cows are very chic with their white coats and black horns. Rather high fashion," she said.

Tristan put a lead on 311 and handed it to me. Mom took it out of my hand and led the calf toward the hitching post while Tristan tied the other lead on 313. The fringe on his suede chaps swayed with his easy gait.

"Gypsy sure is beautiful," Mom said.

Gypsy's nose twitched as I searched my pocket for a sugar cube. Mom took the treat from me and fed it to Gypsy.

"Now we've got two women on this ranch feeding the animals sugar. She's not gonna want to get back to work. Saddling her up wasn't exactly easy. There was quite the dance until I mentioned the race," Tristan said.

"Somebody on this ranch has to be soft," I replied.

"Is that what you think you are?" Tristan set his foot in the stirrup and saddled up. "Dang, girl, you're as tough as they get."

"You're right about that," Mom said. "She doesn't give up easily."

"That's an understatement," Tristan added.

The babies rolled over with a swift kick to the ribs. Tristan's grin flatlined as I held the sides of my belly.

"You okay?" He took the calves' leads from my mother and tied them to his saddle.

My stomach rolled like the ocean. Mom held me steady. "Geez, did I do this to you?"

"Afraid so. You moved a lot right before you were born. I could've sworn you tap-danced on my bladder twenty-four hours a day those last few weeks."

Tristan's gaze dimmed. The rich hue of his black saddle reflected his intensity. He told the calves it was time to go back to the pasture. His tone meant business.

"I'm sure they'll be back," I said.

"Without a doubt," he replied. He adjusted his cowboy hat and continued his conversation with the two runaways. He and Gypsy strolled down the path toward the towering pines. Her tail swished with his easy stride. He'd obviously come to an agreement with her. I suspected getting her to call a truce meant patience and time talking about a reward for good behavior.

"Being tough comes from your father's side of the family," Mom said. "He was always hard on himself. Suppose he still is."

"He's determined, for sure. He has high expectations for himself. For everyone."

"Is he tough on Maggie?"

Intuition told me to tread lightly. There wasn't any reason to take sides. "Yes," I answered, wanting to keep everyone on an even playing field.

"Your eyes tell me something different, Chloe Jean."

"Sometimes. But his soft spot for Maggie keeps him on an even keel. Makes life better for all of us. They're a good team. He's focused, knows what he wants to accomplish, knows what it takes to keep this place above water. Maggie makes sure he doesn't work too hard even though working hard comes naturally." I sauntered back up the stairs to the house.

"That was quite the speech." Mom held the door for me. "I know how important Maggie and your father are to you. I should know better than to ask questions like that. You've learned a lot about running this place from your dad and Winston. Your father tells me you keep everyone in line now that you're the foreman." Mom shut the mudroom door behind her.

"I do." I stood a little taller. "Matt's got cattle of his own now. They're doing well, and he's got plans to buy more next spring. I'm not the only one benefiting from Dad and Grandpa's expertise. Dad offered Matt the position of co-CEO. He's business-minded and has agreed to let Dad know when he's ready to take on the position full-time." I leaned against the counter. The sunlight caught the silver horseshoe hanging above Mom's head. "Did you hang that back up?"

"I knew you'd have tools in the drawer. You are your father's daughter." Mom rolled up her sleeves. "Chloe—" She smoothed back a strand of hair that fell against her chiseled cheek.

"Yes," I said, wondering if she'd ever give up the touches of plastic surgery. She was beautiful without them.

"I'm thankful you're tough and determined."

"You're pretty determined yourself," I said. "I like that about us."

MOM, MAGGIE, AND Glad spent the afternoon shopping. No doubt Mom would find things to fill the empty suitcase she'd brought. I stayed home to finish up paperwork for Dad, checked the recent invoices, and arranged Sway's transportation with Tristan. Focusing proved difficult after my talk with my mother. Mom had taken my setback in stride, and I wasn't sure how to handle her acceptance. Playing defense all these years hadn't prepared me for the give-and-take needed to find balance.

I clipped the radio from the kitchen counter to my waistband, then tied my bandanna around my head. The quiet house was too quiet, and there was only so much resting I could do. Maggie had given me a camera and a crash course in photography when I couldn't ride anymore. I used it to take photos of the cattle, horses, and wranglers. Perusing the images on the camera screen at the end of the day became habit, a way to immerse myself into the life I'd been sidelined from. I took my camera from the mantel and checked the battery life.

Lola sat at my feet. She wagged her tail and raised a paw. I fed her a piece of elk jerky from the treat jar on the kitchen counter. After she trotted away, I tore another jerky stick into bite-sized chunks and tucked them in my pocket. I slung the canvas satchel hanging by the mudroom door across my body and filled it with apples, carrots, and cattle cubes. Lola barked and scratched to get out.

"I'm coming." I dropped a handful of sugar cubes into the bag, too. Lola scooted out the door before I could get it fully open. "Hello there, Samson. I'd pet you, but my belly is in the way." He licked my hand, and I fed the hound the jerky he begged for.

A delivery truck pulled up to the house. Before the driver could get out, I gestured for him to roll down the window.

"Got a piece of furniture for a"—he checked his paperwork—"Trout. That's all it says. A one-named cowboy. Figures."

Trout didn't need a last name. He was a legend. "You're at the wrong house. Follow the drive back out to the main road, turn left. It's the next drive. Look for the sculpted bird perched in the iron circle above the gateway."

Calves 311 and 313 stopped grazing along the fence line long enough to listen to the conversation. I wasn't sorry they'd managed to find their way to me again, even if it meant listening to Tristan gripe.

On our walk to the barn, Lola circled the calves and barked. "Come on, girls." I clicked my tongue against the roof of my mouth and held out my hand to them. Calf 311 wandered over first, and 313 followed. We lollygagged down the dirt road. Samson, pleased with my slow stride, puffed out his chest and stayed by my side. I rolled up my sleeves and undid another button as the unusual May temperature rose.

Lola kept us all together in her usual fashion. The thistle grew thick along the edge of the road. I zoomed in on the prickly plant I found alluring and snapped a photo while 313 nudged my knapsack of treats with her nose. Her pleading stare made for a candid shot and could easily find its way into the coffee-table book Maggie was working on. If I didn't know better, the calf was part hound. My grandfather's bond with the white cattle lived on through me.

I was Montana bred.

These cattle weren't your average Angus. They harnessed a mystery tied to the past, their journey to the States an effort to keep the breed intact during World War II. Their legacy maintained by sheer hardiness. Something I related to.

We lingered in the empty field near the stream. "Come on, 313." She stuck her nose in my knapsack, almost knocking me over. "Patience and manners," I said. "Those words are for all of us." She took the apple from the palm of my hand like a greedy horse. While she munched, I ambled ahead with 311.

Trout lugged a bale of hay from the barn. I shaded my eyes at the man who'd put himself in charge of me when I didn't behave. I glanced down at Lola. "I knew you weren't working solo." She barked and scooted beneath the fence rail.

"Kid, you should be off your feet."

"Nice to see you, too. Can't spend the whole afternoon with my feet up. Not my style. What can

I do to buy your silence?"

"Not a man to be bought."

"Nor penned in or tied down," I added.

"Nope. Looks like you've got yourself a crew."

"The best crew a girl could ask for. So what gives with the delivery, cowboy?"

"Snooping, are we?"

"It's not snooping when the truck ends up at my house." A squawking bird circled. "Hey, if you're here, who's gonna let them in?"

"Instructions are on the porch. If they botch it, I know where to find some capable men."

"What did you buy?"

"You sure are curious."

"Always." Butch and Sundance, two sandy drafts, trotted over to the fence. "Let me see those hindquarters. Have you been staying out of the burrs?" I gave them carrots after inspecting their tails.

"Double trouble is doing their best." Trout went into the barn for another bale of hay.

I used to admire big families with all the aunts, uncles, cousins, and grandparents. I thought I was missing out, but my perspective had changed. People were people. Families were derived from those who loved each other, not necessarily common genetics.

Trout dropped the hay near the gate and stared at me. I lifted the camera to my eye and snapped his picture.

"Speaking of double trouble, how's your momma?"

"Had an info dump at breakfast. Still processing it. She's complicated. She sent more furniture. Her retail binges aren't necessary. You're not gonna say anything, are you?"

"Nope." He opened the gate.

Shrill caws interrupted the conversation. "Looks like the essence of Frankie, my old friend the crow, lives on. Do you remember him?"

"It's been buzzing my tower for the last hour. And yes, I remember Frankie. You nursed that noisy bird back to health your first summer here." Trout rubbed his chin. "You'd named all the barn cats and charmed the horses in no time. You were home, darlin'."

"Yes, I was." The crow landed and paced along the pond's shoreline. "Maybe if you listen to its message, it'll go away."

"Will it now?"

"I'm serious. It's not squawking 'bout nothing," I said. "What's it saying to you?"

Trout hauled the bales into the pasture and placed them beneath the shade tree. I shut the gate and followed.

"I don't know what it's saying, and I've done plenty of listening. Time for it to move on." He took a black feather from his pocket.

"Your tone suggests otherwise. Did you know a black feather can be a gift of wisdom? If you remain open-minded, insight will come your way."

"The message must be for you," Trout said.

"Thanks." I tucked the feather behind my ear.

The bird cocked its head and watched us.

"Darn bird." Trout snagged his fishing rod leaning against the tree, checked his reel, then walked the perimeter of the pond, talking to himself.

I fiddled with my bandanna. Lola waded into the water, her sights set on catching a healthy trout of her own. I held the camera to my eye, zoomed in, and captured a close-up of Trout. The sun kissed his cheeks, his serious gaze like a book cover, protecting his story.

He inspected the flies he'd stuck into the flap of his shirt pocket. Not satisfied with any of them, he unlatched the hook on a wooden box no bigger than the palm of his hand. It contained lures, hooks, tweezers, and a pair of silver scissors that shone like glitter in the daylight.

"My messes don't resemble any of your lures."

I pointed to the Woolly Bugger. "Use that one. It has the best name," I said.

Trout fingered the flies. "Tying flies is an art, and your *knotted messes* work just fine. You underestimate yourself."

"I wouldn't give me that much credit."

"Your intricate web holds us all together."

I shifted my weight, trying to get comfortable.

Trout attached the fly to the end of his line. I snapped another picture.

"You ain't doing much sitting. Why don't you put the camera down and grab a pole? It's been a while since I've seen you work your magic."

"What's the wager?"

"Whoever catches the most doesn't have to cook," he said.

I grabbed my pole. "Hey! This rod is already rigged, and I don't see my favorite fly in the box."

He snickered. "You didn't think I was gonna give you an advantage, did you?"

"How'd you know I'd be joining you?"

"'Cause you always manage to show up when it's about time to relax."

"You got no chance, cowboy."

"I never did."

I waddled to the pond's bank and whipped my fishing pole back and forth, finding an easy rhythm. Trout set his line, and we listened to the sounds of Mother Nature. Her tune settled what stirred my overthought relationship with my mother.

Trout pulled in the first fish and put the pudgy swimmer on a stringer. He rolled up his sleeves and checked the position of the sun. I reeled in my line and handed him my pole.

"We should probably resume this wager when I'm feeling like myself again, and then you'd have something to crow about." Trout's dark gaze was as gentle as the day I met him. "Sorry. I don't mean to disappoint you."

"Kid, you've never disappointed me." He released the fish he'd strung back into the pond. "I've already caught enough for dinner. I'll walk you home. You don't look so good."

TROUT TOOK OFF his boots and propped his feet on the living room ottoman. Before I counted to ten, he placed his cowboy hat over his face and snored. Lola eyed me as I left the room and went upstairs.

Soon the empty hall would be filled with baby sounds, baby smells, and banter between Matt and me.

I went into Mom's bedroom, sat on the bed,

fluffed her pillow, and sniffed the bottle of perfume on the nightstand. I leafed through the pages of her sketchbook, the wispy drawings of blouses, accessories, hats, and skirts precise and unique. Curly script noted stitching, beads, fabric swatches, and knit details and patterns on each drawing. Several pieces were marked with unexplained asterisks.

Her colors and new ideas were as appealing as the spread in *La Chic*.

I leaned against the headboard, closed my eyes, and pictured myself wrapped in one of her stylish shawls, the shearling collar warm against my neck on a snowy day.

When I opened my eyes, Mom brushed hair away from my cheeks. I'd dreamed of moments like this when I was younger, and I'd remember this one for a long time. "Hi, Mom. How was Bozeman?"

"Got some nice things. New boots." She smiled. "I'm glad you had a chance to rest."

"How long have I been sleeping?" I sat up and fluffed the pillow.

"I don't know. Trout left about an hour ago when I got home." She organized the sticky notes on the desk.

"I didn't mean to disturb your things. The door

was open, and I saw your sketchbook. How'd you learn so much about fashion?"

"By watching, working with designers, took classes. When I was a teenager, I saved my allowance for sketchbooks and fashion magazines. I spent hours in my room drawing models and clothing."

"I never knew."

"I never shared." She patted my hand.

"How come?"

"Because that was a long time ago. I didn't think you'd be interested in hearing about how I'd draw for hours and hours, and dress up, do my makeup—which my mother disapproved of. She was okay with a little blush or lip gloss, but when it came to bold colors, mascara, dark eyeliner, and glitter, she'd hand me the soap and escort me to the sink. I hid the things she disliked most beneath a loose floorboard in my closet. I learned to do my makeup at school and wash before I came home."

"Sneaky."

"I guess so. In high school, I signed my name with an *e* at the end, thought it made me more sophisticated and French." Mom wrapped her hair in a chignon and secured it with a carved, tapered wooden dowel from the nightstand.

"You're always so put together."

"Not always."

An awkward silence fell between us. The impulse to ask her if she got along with Maggie and Gladiola fell to the wayside. "You had a good time shopping?"

"Yes. We ate lunch at a trendy sidewalk restaurant, then hit the boutiques and shops. Glad hasn't changed one bit. She showed me Maggie's coffee-table book in the bookstore. I even bought it."

Maggie had spent years taking photos and using her artistic eye to chronicle Montana ranch life. We were all so proud of her for getting her work published.

"You're being so *normal*. Thank you." I glanced at her feet. "Are those your new boots?"

"I went for flashy." She raised her flared denim hem.

"You usually do. Red as a male cardinal. Wow-wee-wow. Shiny, too."

"Very shiny. And I do have my moments. Thanks for noticing."

"Sure thing." The pressure of the babies weighed on my back. "I tried to fish this afternoon, but I couldn't stand very long. These babies are too much." I fell back against the pillow. "I don't want to do this."

"Kissing a cowboy has its consequences."

"Subtle, Mom."

"You're not the only one with habits to break. You're also not the only one in this room who's kissed a cowboy."

I wiggled to the edge of the bed. "Will you help me get up? I'm stuck, and it's time for dinner."

Mom hooked her arm with mine and pulled with a hidden heft. The hint of her perfume tickled my nose. Not quite ready to acknowledge my mother's essence, my choice of words made expressing my true feelings easier. Keeping a safe distance would cushion later disappointment should history repeat itself.

"Thanks for telling me *your* stories. You should meet my mom. She's stubborn, a real go-getter. Knows what she wants but has a hidden side. I don't think she realizes that the best gifts don't always come from the pocketbook. Those are my favorite surprises."

"You should meet my daughter. She's about to have the time of her life. She's spunky, thinks hiding her hurt will keep those around her from hurting, too, can manage a crew of cowboys, and has grown to be quite the woman. She's beautiful inside and out."

CHAPTER 8

D AD ROCKED IN his favorite chair on the porch of the main house as Mom and I climbed the steps. "Brook," he said with a nod. "I hear you ladies had a successful day of shopping."

"We did." Her reply was clipped.

"She didn't buy me any more furniture. That's a win-win," I said. "I really appreciate the constraint, Mom. I'm proud of you."

My parents kept their conversations to a minimum when they were together. I was never quite sure how to break the ice. As usual, I stood between them, tongue-tied and unsure how to intervene.

"We should join the others," I said, opening the front door.

Laughter erupted from inside. We made our way to the kitchen to join the crew.

Matt entered from the mudroom, his bright eyes and dimples were exactly what I needed. He took off his cowboy hat and hung it on one of the hand-forged hooks made from railroad spikes mounted on the wall. "Sounds like a party in here."

"Trout's telling stories." Maggie laughed and tossed a leafy green salad.

"They ain't stories, honey."

Maggie patted him on the back and handed Dad a platter of fish. "Would you mind taking this into the dining room?" She winked at him and then included my mom. "Brook, could you dress the salad? I used the lo-cal balsamic recipe you suggested. It's delicious."

I envied Maggie's easiness in handling my parents when we were together. She held them accountable with a fair disposition. She handed me an artsy ceramic dish detailed with painted sparrows peeking out from beneath the mound of potato salad.

"Well, there she is," Trout said. He poured Mom a glass of white wine and handed it to her. She swished the wine like a sommelier and sniffed it.

I introduced Matt to my mom. He shook her hand and didn't miss a beat when it came to apologizing for missing last night's dinner. "I hear you had quite the time in town today. If we can get John to play us a tune on his daddy's guitar tonight, maybe you'd like to kick up a little dust with a dance move or two."

"That might be nice." Mom sipped her wine.

"Someone's not shy." Maggie ushered us all out of the kitchen. "Dinner awaits."

"Tristan will be here shortly. The other fellas are heading down the road to the diner. Tristan's not one for whooping it up over beers on a Friday evening. He'd rather settle in for the night around a table of family." Matt pulled out Mom's chair.

The table was set with Maggie's vintage collection of china, each place setting different from the next. The varying shades of reds and pinks reminded me of a rose garden. After we gave thanks, conversation came easily. Trout and Dad chatted about fishing. Matt discussed his schooling, how he met me, and the cattle with my mom. Glad entertained Tristan with her charming banter and corny jokes.

Mom polished off a glass of wine and nodded to Trout for a refill.

Glad gushed about all the cute baby items they saw while shopping, and then she called my mother Grannie Brook, which brought the dinner conversation to a halt.

"I'm glad you brought that up." Mom squared her shoulders.

"Oh boy," I said between sips of water.

"I'd like the babies to call me Coco."

Matt's stunned appearance prompted smiles from Maggie and Glad. Mom's surprises would be never-ending. Her request was milder than I expected.

"And Coco's staying for eight weeks," I said.

Mom raised her glass for a toast. We all joined in, playing along.

We were a modern family.

THE STARS FLICKERED overhead in the indigo sky. Flames from the bonfire popped and sparked. Dad strummed his guitar and sang a country Montana tune. Mom sipped wine and inspected her Montana boots which came with a designer price tag. Maggie zipped up her oilskin jacket and settled into the old Adirondack chair. She propped her feet on the log, her dreamy gaze focused on Dad.

Mom caught my stare and raised her glass to me.

Matt's shoulder brushed mine as he leaned closer to the embers to toast a marshmallow, the glow accentuating his strong jaw. "Let it go, Chloe," he whispered. "We had a nice dinner. It's time to unwind."

I compared Matt's profile with my dad's. They

both preferred a scruffy chin of whiskers. Their broad shoulders a testament to their demeanors, strength, and work ethic.

I held a graham cracker in each hand, ready to intercept the gooey pillow of sugar. "Delicious. Ranks right up there with a hot pickle and beef sandwich."

Matt threaded two more marshmallows on the skewer, then stuck them into the fire. They burst into flames, and he jerked his hand back and blew them out with a grin. "My kind of perfection."

"I should say so," Dad interjected into the lyrics of the song. "Carbonized marshmallow beats those sandwiches you've been eating—any day."

I pointed a finger at Dad. "Oh, I don't think so, Dad, and way better than sticky char. So gross," I said through a mouthful.

Dad nodded at Matt, who threaded more marshmallows onto the skewer while Dad finished his song. Matt held them over the fire carefully until Dad set his guitar back in the case.

"I'll give you the honors, sir." Matt handed the skewer to Dad.

Dad took in Maggie's silly smile, then let the golden marshmallows burst into flames. With one quick puff, he blew out the inferno. "That's my favorite part. Never gets old," he said.

Maggie shook her head. She loved my dad to the moon and back, silly antics and all.

"So you do enjoy spontaneous combustion. I'll remember that," I said.

My mom chuckled into her wineglass.

"Matt's got a surprise for you, Chloe. Now's as good a time as any, son." Dad handed Matt the guitar.

"If it's a surprise like Lola, bring it on. If it's a surprise like the twins, show me later—way later. Although, I can't imagine you'll ever top that."

"I most certainly can, girl." Matt's Southern drawl was spot on. His fingers picked a familiar tune, one we'd listened to many times in college. Matt strummed the chords to one of his favorites about lost friends and old loves under an autumn moon. He loved his music.

Dad stood and offered Maggie his hand. She took it, and he pulled her into his arms. Mom accepted Trout's invite, and they joined in the dance. Watching the four of them sway to the music took my breath away.

Matt didn't end the song like I'd heard on the original recording; he repeated the last phrase, then sang the chorus again.

At the end of his rendition, Matt returned the guitar to Dad's chair, held out his hand, and I took it. "That was pretty terrific." I stood and fell into his arms with no grace whatsoever. "When did you learn to play the guitar?"

"I've been learning for a while. Tristan's a good teacher."

"He is, huh? Seems that guy knows more than he lets on."

"We all have hidden talents. What do you say I get you home? Once you have those babies, we'll talk about dancing," Matt said.

"Every day is a dance in my book," I replied. Matt exuded cowboy from head to toe. There was nothing more appealing than a man who wrangled horses, cows, and sometimes me.

"Yes, it is, darlin'. And that's why you're my girl."

Maggie and Dad said good night. Trout and Mom settled into their respective seats and chatted about California. Mom sipped her wine. The evening light made it difficult to see how much was left in the bottle. Her giggle suggested she'd had enough. Matt tugged at my hand. "We'll take the long way home."

Lola nipped at the hem of my jeans. "You can come, too," I told her. She stared up at me with her dark eyes, her pink tongue waggling.

"I know what you mean, Lola," Matt said,

patting his thigh. Lola woofed, did a figure eight between Matt's legs, spun in a circle, then jumped into his arms.

"What's with you two? You got treats in your pocket?"

"Nope. That would be you. We're just playing. Come on now. Your mom can handle herself."

"I hope so," I said.

Mom's half-masted gaze was focused on Trout. He told fly-fishing tales, and she listened. Trout didn't seem to mind the company. He nodded in my direction; he'd escort her home.

Lola jumped from Matt's arms. Her white shaggy fur danced as she trotted ahead. "Thanks for the song." I squeezed Matt's hand. His sweet side wasn't hidden as deep as my father's. When he let it shine, the world was right. "Don't tell Dad I said this, but you play better than he does, and he's been doing it a lot longer."

"I'll take that compliment." A dim bulb glowed behind the seam of the barn doors at the end of the dirt road we walked along. The echo of Gypsy's loping stride across the pasture was unmistakable. I strained to see her.

"Hi, girl. I came to say good night." I patted the tuft of mane between her ears, then stroked her velvety nose.

Matt rested his elbow on the fence rail, and Gypsy nibbled at his jacket. She snorted and pawed at the ground.

"That's my cue to get you home, Momma."

"Matt, how did your family know your brother, Kibby, had a drinking problem?" I took his hand, and we headed back to the house.

"Who has a problem?"

"My mother, perhaps."

"Chloe, she's been here a hot minute. You haven't seen her in a long time. She's out of her element." He shrugged. "You've got to hand it to her. She's staying on her ex-husband's property in an area of the country that's far from what she's used to. Not to mention, she's trying to hold it together for her daughter. She's nothing like my brother. His binges are reckless and regular. He'd drink morning, noon, and night if he could. Hides it, doesn't hide it. Jail time. The drinking certainly changed him. Sad thing is, I couldn't tell what drove him to it. I know you don't want to hear this, but don't make a mountain out of something you're not sure of."

The lights of the house glowed. My mother and Trout were in the living room, standing near the fireplace engaged in conversation. They appeared to be enjoying each other's company.

"She says she's lonely. I didn't know she felt that way. She's always with someone, working, scheduled for an appointment or meeting."

"Some people do a great job of hiding it. Being active doesn't mean she's not lonely."

Watching her, I whispered, "I suppose."

"Give her time to settle in. Give her a chance." Matt rubbed his chin. "The house sure looks great."

"Yes, it does. The babies will like it here."

"Correction. The babies will *love* it here."

"What are Mom and Trout doing?" I pointed at the scene unfolding in the living room. "Oh my Lord!" I tugged at Matt's hand. "She's kissing Trout." I couldn't look away. "Make it stop. Make it stop."

Trout took my mother by the shoulders and backed away.

"Oh boy." Matt knocked his hat back and relaxed his stance.

"This can't be happening. Aren't you going to say or do anything? Why is this happening? I can't just stand here."

Matt stepped around me, blocking my view of the house. He put his hand on my shoulder and held my gaze.

"Yes, you can," he said. "And you know what

you shouldn't do?"

"What?" I rested my hands on my belly.

"Get crazy over a situation you can't control."

"Thanks for being supportive." I planted my hands on my hips with a huff. "First, she shows up early. Then she says she's staying for eight weeks, and now this. She's been here two days. You're right about one thing. I can't control this, but I can get in the middle of it."

Matt sighed and scratched his head. "First Gypsy. Now you. Good night, Chloe."

"Really? She shouldn't be kissing Trout. He's off limits. He's like my grandpa. She has no boundaries. How will I look him in the eye? Or her? I'm trying my best here to put *us*"—I used air quotes around the word *us*—"back together. You're just gonna say good night and walk away?"

He took his hat off and fiddled with the brim. "I am. I don't see how it's my place to get in the middle. I'll be up for a bit if you need to call. Good night, babies." He kissed his fingers and touched my belly. Matt's silhouette faded into the night as he walked away.

Mom's visit was supposed to be about me, the babies, and reuniting. She'd flipped a switch and exposed me to something I didn't want any part of. This was more than a step backward. And Trout—

what was he thinking?

I marched up the back steps, went inside, and made sure the door slammed behind me. My footsteps were extra heavy through the mudroom and into the kitchen. I opened the fridge and rattled the contents before entering the living room.

What I saw contradicted what I'd seen from a distance.

"Hey, kid," Trout said.

Mom wiped her nose with a tissue. Her eyes were red.

"What's wrong?" Why was she crying? What had happened between them?

Trout said good night to my mother, then I walked him to the back door after neither one of them answered me.

"Trout."

"Yeah, kid."

"I could pretend I didn't see anything, but I know what I saw. I also know you don't like discussing women, but this time it's different. It involves my mother. I deserve an explanation." I followed him through the kitchen.

He didn't say anything.

"Why were you kissing?"

He pushed the screen door open in the mudroom and left.

"Hey," I called after him as he walked into the night toward his cabin. I took off my bandanna and scrunched it up. After shutting the door, I went back to the living room to hear mom's explanation, but she'd already gone upstairs. Her broken wineglass on the hearth was the only clue to what had happened.

I picked up the black feather Trout had given me from the mantel. Keeping an open mind about my mom and Trout's kiss would be impossible. Clearly, there would be no explanation tonight. I'd sweep up the glass, turn down the lights, and review the photos on my camera in hopes of gaining peace of mind before closing my eyes.

CHAPTER 9

TWO DAYS HAD come and gone. Mom was holed up in her room doing business long distance, and I followed as much of my routine as I could. I called Maria, nanny option number two, and left another message. I'd cleaned everything there was to clean and reorganized the closets when I wasn't watching the wranglers from behind the wheel of Grandpa's old truck.

Nothing I did erased what I had seen. Mom had kissed Trout, and his quick exit hadn't hidden the fury behind his eyes.

I knocked on the front door of Trout's cabin and waited properly for him to answer, something I didn't usually do. The honey-colored wood had reddish highlights, and the timber-framed windows were drape-free, letting in the light and my roving eye. When the paneled front door opened, I was greeted with a click of his tongue.

"I hope it's okay that I'm here. I haven't seen you around. Thought I should check on you."

"I expected you before now."

"I haven't seen you since—well, you know. And I'm not running away. So please don't ask if I am."

Trout invited me into the living room. He sat in an upholstered chair I hadn't seen before. I stood there, trying to make sense of the situation. Trout's home was inviting and cozy. Everything Montana and loving. The logs hewn from Virginia timbers had been restored to a chestnut hue. The fieldstone chimney reached the vaulted ceiling of exposed beams. Antlers he'd collected as a boy, family trinkets, and books lined the shelves. The rustic chandelier glowed with warm yellow light.

"Nice chair. Is that what the delivery was all about?"

"Yep."

"I like the pattern. The light blue background reminds me of the Montana summer sky and the sunflowers of warm fields that stretch for miles." Trout fingered the armrests and put his feet up on the matching ottoman.

"You sure you're not running away? Your people are probably wondering where you are."

"If anyone understands running away, it's my mother. She's been in her room for the better of two days. And I'm sure I'm not running. In fact, I was a little scared to come here, because I think you're hiding out, too."

"I understand. And I don't know anyone who doesn't run away from something. We all have baggage. Even me, especially now." He took his cowboy hat off and tossed it toward the bleached antler hat rack mounted on the wall. His hat fell to the ground.

"You gonna pick that up?" I asked.

"Nope. You sound like my momma."

"Sorry."

"No need to be sorry. Just letting you know you're headed in the right direction."

"What happened, Trout? Between you and Mom."

"Your momma's carrying a heavy load, kid. She has always overpacked and is overzealous 'bout other people's business. Nothing's changed about her since the day I met her."

"Comes naturally. You should know that by now. Did she kiss you?" I took in Trout's sour expression.

"I *do* know, and I ain't discussing what happened with your momma."

"It's hard to be mad at you."

"Is it?" He lifted a bushy brow.

I nodded. "This is her. I know it."

"You momma's actions aren't your doing."

"She initiated the kiss, didn't she? I'd feel better if she did."

Trout laced his fingers and rested his hands in his lap.

"You're not talking, are you?"

"Nope. Like I said, she's lost. I know it doesn't feel like it now, and it may never feel like it, but she needs you."

"You sure about that?"

"I'm sure." Trout's moustache twitched.

"Didn't think I'd have to hold my mother's hand. She's always been independent."

"Sometimes parents need that sort of thing."

"Parents are supposed to be the rock." My breath caught in my chest. "Oh gosh, it's my turn to be the rock."

"Rocks need moving from time to time. They can't always roll on their own."

"Who knew?" I rubbed my temples. "The babies. They're gonna want to move me. I don't like being moved unless it's my idea."

"You got that right. Your daddy did plenty of moving your granddaddy when he was alive. Nobody knows until it's their time to do the rolling. Parents can't always be the wind at your back, kid."

"This adulting is a tall order."

"Yep. And I got news for you. No one ever stops growing. People are like wildflowers. They can be pulled out by the roots and grow back. Most of the time when you least expect it."

"You gonna sit for a spell or go home?"

"I haven't decided."

"Your boots are mighty fancy."

"My mom gave them to me last year for my birthday. I thought I'd give them a try. Thought maybe walking in her boots, so to speak, would help me understand, give me a different perspective."

"She's got good taste."

"Yes, she does."

I thought I saw a slight smile. He glanced at the built-in bookshelves.

"I hear you and Silas have quite the discussions about cowboy literature," I said.

"Mostly literature in general. Reading nurtures the soul. You read the books I share with you but don't say much when you're done."

"Guess not. I'm too busy thinking about the story and why it's important to you."

"It's not about me. It's about you. A story might carry a different meaning for you than it does for me."

"I'll remember that for the next read." I perused the bookshelf. I ran my fingers across the book spines as I inspected them, searching for the one meant for me.

"Take what you want."

"What I want isn't on this shelf."

"Didn't think so."

I chose a vintage chapter book and opened the cover. Trout had written his name in crude loopy letters on the inside at the noted age of ten. A scrap of paper from between the pages fell to the floor. I picked it up and tucked it in the book before putting the book back.

"Appreciate that." He nodded with a wink.

"Trout—" I glanced at him.

"We ain't talking about women."

"How did you know I was gonna ask?"

"Call it intuition. I've told you before and I'll tell you again, I'm not discussing women with you."

"But—"

"Ain't no buts, kid."

"Guess me knowing would take some of the fun out of our sparring matches."

"Sure would."

I took in the black-and-white photos framed in rough wood on the timber mantel and stepped closer to see them better. "You look like your dad."

"Yep."

"He was handsome."

"Guess that makes me handsome, too." Trout scratched his head, then ran his hands through his thick, white hair. "I ain't discussing my past with you. And if you plan on staying any longer, we best change the subject."

I sat on the leather sofa and propped my feet up on the ottoman. Trout and I stared at each other. I imagined him as a young man.

"You would've been a great father."

"I told you—"

"I know what you told me. I wanted you to know what I was thinking."

"Why is it that people today think everyone wants to hear what they're *thinking*? People like you and me don't always need words. Sometimes just being should be wisdom enough."

"Kind of like osmosis."

"You're killing the vibe, kid." He crossed his arms over his chest.

I knew what he meant. Our connection was created by something bigger than the both of us. His spiritual nature was surfacing. I crossed my arms over my chest, too, picturing the knotted angst in the pit of my stomach drifting into the universe. "Do you think—?"

Trout put his pointer finger to his lips.

I did the same and blew out the words that were on the tip of my tongue.

Trout held up five fingers, then pointed to the grandfather clock in the corner of the room. He'd told me once that the clock belonged to his grandmother and its soft chime was like her voice calling him home. At the stroke of three, he closed his eyes. The slightest of smiles crept into the seam of his lips; I imagined he was revisiting a different time.

Not talking for five minutes would be tough. I'd talked my whole life. Listening took more energy than voicing every passing thought. I suspected Trout's philosophy about listening would likely solve many world problems.

My mind reeled. I didn't want Trout or my mother to hide away. What was the sense in that? I pushed them from my thoughts, closed my eyes, too, and daydreamed of picking wildflowers and braiding them into Gypsy's silky mane.

"You awake, kid?"

When I opened my eyes, Trout stood before me with the book I'd taken from the shelf and put back. "Something drew you to this classic. I bought it at a garage sale for a nickel, a long time ago. A story I read many times as a youngster. You should take it. I know you're busy and it might be a while before I see it again, but I'm okay with that. If I need it, I know where to find it. Could be the distraction you've been looking for." He patted my shoulder. "It's time you should be going."

I glanced at the clock. Trout helped me get to my feet.

"Five minutes. That's all it takes if you let yourself relax," Trout said.

I took the book. The title was faded and the pages too. The inscription inside read:

From Aunt Alma to Marguerite
September 8, 1915

I didn't know what the story was about, but I didn't question Trout's choice. I didn't have to. He'd always had that effect on me, and I'd do well to trust him now. Any book with a handwritten inscription must be special.

"Thanks, Trout."

"You're welcome, kid."

I stood at the door. Over my shoulder was a man who'd spent his life learning in a different way than I had. "I suspect whenever I visit, it'll come with a lesson like it did when I was a child."

"You suspect right. Could you please—?"

"Yes. I'll shut the door quietly behind me.

That's one lesson I've mastered."

"Good girl." He clicked his teeth.

"Speaking of girls, can't you just tell me the color of her hair or where she lived?"

"Nope."

Trout shooed me away like he did when I was a little girl and didn't want to go home. I stepped outside, making sure the screen door didn't slam shut.

"I can come back whenever I want, right?" A question he'd heard many times.

He peered through the screen door. "Always. Now, scat."

I shuffled across the porch thinking, Trout and I had been cut from the same rugged cloth. We were rough around the edges, but when we loved, we loved hard. I waved goodbye, then made my way down the path, through the grove of pines, and back home.

CHAPTER 10

I'D GOTTEN UP without an alarm before sunrise. From behind the wheel of Grandpa's truck near the corral, I watched the men round up the horses from the mountainside across the open field. Gypsy led the herd, her wild canter furious against the ground, like the sky had opened up with an unexpected storm. Before entering the pasture, she reared up with a squeal. Matt dismounted and tied Trigger to the hitching post, fanned away dust clouds, and shot me an *I told you so* look.

I'd invited Mom along for the ride this morning, but she claimed not to be ready when I left the house. As much as I wanted to know what happened with Trout, I wanted her to ride shotgun even more.

I opened the truck door as Silas rode up on Cisco. Getting unwedged from behind the steering wheel took effort.

"Hey, Silas. That was very sweet of you to send the poetry book, and thanks for oiling this door."

"You're welcome, and you can keep the book if

you want. I have plenty more."

"Thanks. By any chance, did Matt tell you we're having a hard time finding a nanny?"

Maria, nanny number two, hadn't returned my call, and no one else had inquired about the position. I was no more than twenty-four hours away from losing my mind over the prospect of being nanny-less.

"Yes, ma'am, he did." Silas stroked his beard. "He also told me I wasn't allowed to entertain any offers that might come my way pertaining to such a position."

"Darn him." I massaged my lower back. "You're good with children, aren't you?"

"My great-aunt ran a daycare. Helping her after school kept me out of trouble."

"I knew it."

Matt sauntered over. "No, Chloe. We need him out here."

Silas laughed. He and I watched Matt walk into the barn.

"Fine, but if I'm ever in a real pinch, could I call you for help?"

"As long as it doesn't cause a strain between you two."

I patted his rock-solid bicep. "Dang, I didn't think it was possible for you to get more muscles."

"I've been doing chin-ups in the old barn. Found the ideal spot. That place is like a sanctuary. Peaceful as all get-out, and when the sun shines through the open door, it's like being served a slice of heaven."

"You're right about that." I tipped my hat. "You're a good man, Silas. I'm glad you're here."

Mom and Maggie chatted outside the barn. Mom crossed her arms and frowned. Maggie kicked at the dirt and tugged at the brim of her cowboy hat. Leaning against the pasture fence, I pretended not to pay attention. Maggie could handle herself. I couldn't help but compare them, the one who gave me life and the one who made sure I stayed alive.

Mom's beauty was magazine unblemished without the airbrushing, Maggie's defined by character and time. Her freckled, careworn skin and slender physique reminded me of the black-and-white photos I'd seen of my grandmother. Ida May and Maggie didn't resemble each other genetically, but their eyes glowed with the same pride and tenacity.

Gypsy wandered over and stuck her nose over the timber fence rail. "Hi, girl. You best behave or they'll find you a pen somewhere." Her ears twitched. "Thanks for cooperating with Tristan.

Your fits won't fly with the others though." She showed me her teeth and shook her head. I fed her the juicy apple I'd tucked in the pocket of my jean jacket.

"Hey, pretty girl." Justin dismounted in a whirl and tied his dappled gray mare, Belle, to the hitching post. "I was talking to Gypsy." He chuckled and patted me on the back. "Tristan may have an in with her, but the rest of us are skating on thin ice in her pond."

Matt joined me at the fence, his dusty chaps snug to his thighs. Gypsy ran off, kicking up fresh dirt.

"Tristan seems to ride her just fine," I said.

"I'm still not riding her or getting close," Matt said. "You saw her tantrum. The longer those babies tie you up, the rougher it gets."

"So you've said." I glanced toward the barn. "Seems Maggie and my mom are having words. Did you mention to anyone that we saw Trout and my mom kissing? Because I didn't." My inquisition was met with an irritated stare. "Did you?"

Matt stepped closer.

"Excuse me? And if I did? Which I didn't, by the way. So much for taking a deep breath and a step back." He wiped his brow. "I know you want everyone to get along. They'll solve their disagreement. Focus on yourself."

Unexpected pain took my breath away. My knees buckled from the surge, and Matt caught me by the elbow. Mom and Maggie cut the conversation and rushed over to me.

"You should get off your feet," Matt said.

"I don't want to." I wiped away the beading sweat on my forehead.

"You okay?" Mom asked.

"Whoa," I moaned. I'd seen cattle, horses, cats, and dogs deliver, and my turn was coming. Fear crept through me, and I pushed it away. "I don't know. They just keep moving." Matt put his hand on the small of my back and led me toward the house. Mom and Maggie coaxed me to breathe. Mom laced her fingers with mine.

"You're not going to break me. Squeeze as tight as you want," she said.

The babies rolled over, and I tightened my grip. The radiating pain didn't make what I had seen or heard since my mother's arrival disappear. "You know what, Mom?"

"What, honey?"

"I could've used more of this hand holding when I was younger."

Matt groaned. "This isn't the time."

"Oh yes, it is. She can't get upset with me

now—there are babies involved."

"It's fine, Matt. Let it out, Chloe. He'll never know what it feels like to push a turkey through his vagina."

"Matt, you'll have to excuse Coco. She has no filter." I held my mother's stare. "Was I really as big as a turkey?"

"Yes, Chloe. The most beautiful turkey ever," she said with a wince. "I remember it like it was yesterday. Nine pounds. Three ounces."

"You two seem suited for each other. Remind me why you can't get along," Matt said.

"You're living on the edge, Cooper." Maggie climbed the steps to the timber-framed front porch of my house and held the door open.

"Come on, darlin'," Matt said, getting me to the living room sofa. "We have to call Dr. Hennessey."

"On it." Maggie made her way to the phone in the kitchen.

"The babies can't come now. I'm not ready."

"You're as ready as you'll ever be," Matt said.

"As much as I want them out of me, it's not time." My eyes brimmed with tears. "I can't do it. Any of it." I held Mom's stare. She understood.

I sat with a thud and squeezed the sofa's armrest. Deep breaths didn't soothe the pain. I kept my next rush of words to myself. I tossed my hat on the ottoman, then tied the black paisley bandanna embroidered with my grandmother's initials around my head. My gaze focused on Matt. "How *hot* am I now?"

"Smokin'." He winked.

"The office notified the doctor. Time the contractions," Maggie said as she joined us in the living room.

Mom slid the bandanna from my head and fingered my hair. "You can do it. I'm here to prove that you can."

"Hey, I need my bandanna."

"You'll feel better without it. This one is kind of grunge rock." She folded it into neat squares, smoothing the fabric with each crease.

Maggie and Matt's gazes connected, my fake smile met with blank stares. "Bet you wish you were me right now. Don't you?"

"I'll get her packed," Maggie said.

"Me or my mother?" My sarcasm was met with frowns. "Sorry. I have to quit doing that." I fanned my cheeks. "I'm packed, and my bag is at the foot of my bed."

Matt rubbed his chin. I knew his frustrated expression well.

"She's been like this since she was a child. I

appreciate your patience with my daughter. I'm afraid I have an adverse effect on her. Being in labor doesn't help."

I cringed at the brewing acid reflux.

"Are you having another contraction?" Matt asked.

"No. Could you get me the bottle of antacids from the kitchen, please?"

Maggie returned with my leather duffel. She peered out the front window and shook her head. "I can't believe it. The calves are in the yard again. Tristan's gonna have a fit when he discovers they're here."

"Rescue me, 311 and 313," I called, letting my feet slide out in front of me. "I'm like a beached whale. The babies are crushing me. They have to find another way out."

"How many minutes has it been?" Maggie asked.

Matt returned with the chalky tablets, then checked the time. "We left the barn twenty minutes ago. You've been upstairs about five."

"It may be my due date, but I'm feeling better now that I'm sitting down. The doctor said Braxton-Hicks contractions can feel very real."

Maggie took the radio from her belt. "I'll be outside if you need me. You got this, Brook?"

LINDA BRADLEY

"I'm not going anywhere," Mom answered.

Matt ran his fingers through his hair and stayed for a solid thirty minutes before going back to the barn. He made me pinky swear that I'd call him if I had another contraction.

"I'm okay. I'll call the doctor back." I rested my head on my mom's shoulder. The scent of her perfume was much nicer than the magazine inserts I coveted that reminded me of her. "I hope having these babies goes smoothly."

"Having a baby is tough," Mom said.

"I'm having two of them."

"You could be carrying triplets, quadruplets, quintuplets, sextup—" Mom held up one more finger with each syllable until she ran out of fingers.

"Okay, I get the message. I'll knock it off. I only wish getting them here was easier." I kicked off my boots, laid down, and stuffed a pillow between my knees.

Mom tucked the studded boots beneath the ottoman with a smile. She handed me back my bandanna. "You're right—you do need this. It's the perfect accessory."

"Thanks, Mom." I took deep, calming breaths as she stroked my hair. I held her bright stare, and the banter between us faded. Despite our pledge to leave the past behind, it would always be part of us. The challenge wasn't to forget it—the challenge was to grow from it. Voiced hurt would pave the way to forgiveness if we could let bygones be bygones.

Mom helped me sit up. She unfolded the bandanna and helped me put it back on. Then she kissed her fingers and touched my cheek.

"It doesn't always have to be an olive branch, daughter."

TRISTAN'S VOICE CARRIED through the empty house as he called my name.

"I'll be there in a minute," I answered from my office. I straightened the papers on the antique pecan desk Mom had bought without telling me. It was definitely more tasteful than the faux bear rug. The desk would be staying.

I meandered into the kitchen to find him scratching his head. "What's the look for?"

"What's going on in here?" he replied.

"I had a couple of contractions earlier. False alarm. I'm just lying low. Did a little cleaning after everyone left me alone." I wiped a smudge from the stove. He ran his fingers over the countertop on his way into the living room.

"There's not a speck of dirt or a thing out of place. You sure you're not practicing housewife skills? Nice rug. That bear's mouth would make a great parking garage for toy cars."

"Very funny." I adjusted my bandanna.

Tristan picked up the camera from the end table, pointed it at me unexpectedly, and snapped a few frames. "I've seen you taking photos around the ranch. The other day you were hunkered down in the old pickup waiting for us to ride by."

"Can't do much else. Taking pictures was Maggie's idea. I've taken hundreds and done nothing with them. She gave me the camera and a crash course on how to use it when the doctor said I couldn't ride anymore."

Tristan set the camera next to Maggie's book on the ottoman.

"Those babies must be coming soon. I haven't seen this since—" His eyes clouded over. "I'm not sure I want to go there," he said.

"Go ahead. I'm much better at listening than I used to be." I made a mental note of that thought for the next time I bantered with my mother.

Tristan appeared conflicted. "Remember when I first got here?"

"How could I forget? We weren't very friendly, but we're past that now." The sentiment was inspiration to be patient with my mom. "What's on your mind? You can tell me." Tristan had been obstinate, standoffish when he joined our crew. I now understood that choosing between reining in past hurt and being candid was a tough choice for him. Yet his integrity complimented his loyalty, and he had grown to be a critical part of the wrangling team.

He plucked the gloves from his back pocket and picked at the fringe. "My wife went through the exact thing you're doing now before she had our son. Our house was spick-and-span. Vivian used to tell me she was nesting. I miss her and James every day."

I rested my hand on his shoulder. The thought of Vivian and James being killed by a drunk driver sent shivers down my spine. "I'm so sorry. I can't even pretend to know what you must feel. When people pass on, it creates holes. Big, fat holes." My mother left holes, too. Holes that I promised myself I'd fill with faith and happy memories this time around. Holes that snuck up on me when I thought I was making progress. Holes I'd caused and yearned to patch.

"What did you come here for?" I asked.

"Thought I'd find two fugitives grazing in the yard, since 311 and 313 seem to have gone astray again. I fixed the fence, and they still found a way out."

"Matt took them back to the pasture earlier. I'm guessing you haven't seen him." I glanced out the window.

Mom neared the house with the two calves on her heels. Tristan and I went outside.

"I hope this makes up for something," Mom said. "Quinn helped me with the leads. He walked us most of the way here, then said he had work to do." She held up a canvas satchel. "He thought if I had cow treats, they'd cooperate."

"I can't believe it." I crossed my arms over my chest.

"I have many talents, dear daughter. And I know how happy the cows make you."

"I'll be damned," Tristan said.

"She's filling the holes." Hair prickled on my nape. I looked to the clouds overhead, hoping to get a glimpse of my grandparents. I was sure Vivian and James were there too.

Tristan skipped down the steps. He held his hand to me, making sure I was steady.

"This baby bump is a hazard," I said.

"They'll be here soon, and when they are, the hazards will be different," he replied.

I rested my hand on his shoulder. He peered at

me, a flash in his dark stare.

"I know it's not any consolation, but I'll always be here for you." A strange expression crossed his face. "What now?" I asked.

"You'll think I'm crazy," he said.

"I know you're crazy, but then again, so are the rest of the people on this ranch. Look at my mom, Hollywood diva gone cow whisperer. Pot stirrer gone country. Who knew? Whatever you're thinking, just say it."

"You sounded like Vivian."

"I don't think you're crazy." My breath caught in my chest.

"I should listen more carefully, more often. Maybe I'd hear her." The corners of his eyes crinkled, and he looked away.

"Listening can be tricky. Mood can be a game-changer. When the sun's right and Gypsy's galloping, the world's okay and I'm open. Her hooves drown out the dark places in my mind. The chaos settles, and I can focus."

Calf 313 nudged Tristan as if to say hello. He patted her head.

"It's hard to stay mad at them. Isn't it?"

"Yup," he answered.

I checked out the faded jeans and the plain white tee my mom had changed into. "What happened to working in your room?"

"I snuck out a while ago. I can't stay in there forever. You were in your office. It sure is nice out today." She lifted her chin to the sun.

"Sure is."

Tristan planted his hands on his hips. "These two calves are a couple of players."

Mom laughed and scratched 311's ears. "Once they get used to you, they're not so skittish."

"Doesn't help that Chloe's taken care of them since they were born," Tristan said.

I leaned into 313 and stroked her cheek. "Us girls need to stick together."

"Yes, we do," Mom said, handing me the satchel of cow treats.

"I guess they're staying." Tristan mounted Hitchcock, his dark Appaloosa with the spotted white rump, named after the place he was born: Hitchcock, Texas. Tristan tugged at the brim of his hat and shook his head at the calves.

"I'll keep an eye on them." I stroked Hitch's speckled crown. "Got my radio on if I need you."

Mom plucked a yellow wildflower and stuck it behind her ear.

"Can you close the gate while I go inside and get something?" I asked her.

"Sure."

I returned with my camera; 311 and 313 huddled together with curious stares. I focused the lens and snapped a few frames. Mom coaxed the calves closer.

She stood between them like they'd known each other a lifetime. Somehow, she'd managed to become part of their world in the short time she'd been here. I'd waited twenty-something years for this moment with her, and she'd tainted it by kissing Trout.

I'd told Trout it was hard to be upset with him, and now was my chance to talk to my mom. If I could manage a group of wranglers, managing myself and how I handled her should have come easier than I'd made it. I picked two purple flowers resembling fireworks. "Early bloomers. Can I weave these into your braid?"

Mom nodded. I worked the spindly stems into her golden hair, then snapped a photo while she absorbed the vast Montana landscape.

"Why'd you kiss Trout?"

Her shoulders fell forward. "I told you, it was a huge misunderstanding on my part. I can honestly say that I don't know what came over me. It shouldn't have happened. I'd had way too much wine. I should've talked to you before now."

"I think you have too much wine most nights."

139

I rested the camera against my chest, taking in her posture and tone as 313 walked away and 311 sidestepped into my mother. She clasped her hands on the back of the calf and stared into the distance. I took their picture. The viewfinder cropped the mountainous backdrop, the fertile valley lush as ever.

"I meant what I said, Chloe. It was a costly misunderstanding. I know it means something to you, but it really didn't mean anything." She kneaded the back of her neck and lowered her lashes. "Being here has stripped away the years. Buried memories are rising like Olympus, and they're rocking me to my core. This house. Seeing your dad and Maggie together. Your life. Thought I'd breeze in, stay awhile. It isn't any easier than keeping my end of our pledge to start new."

"Eight weeks is more than awhile, Mom. We can't fix everything all at once and now this. I don't get why you kissed Trout. Are you attracted to him?" My heart raced.

"No."

"Then why? I can't wrap my brain around it. We don't need another *thing* between us."

"I understand. And you're right. *We don't need another thing between us.*" She stroked the calf's back. "Seeing you kick off the boots I gave you made me so happy." She sighed. "Once upon a time, I stood in this very spot on your father's arm. Being here reminds me of everything I let go."

"You made a choice."

"I also made a choice to come back because I need you in my life." Her eyes teared up.

I'd never seen my mother cry. I took a deep breath and gave her a minute to collect herself. I closed the gap between us and held her hand.

"I wanted to be here for you, and as usual, I'm not. I've made a spectacle of myself. You think I've invaded your private space, which I have. You also think I'm gunning for the older hired hand, which I'm not." Mom pushed her shoulders back. "And that I drink too much, which I might at times."

"I'm worried about you."

"I appreciate your concern, but there's really nothing to worry about. I shouldn't have to convince you I don't have a problem. Chloe, I've got my therapist and friends. I'm not a case for you to fix. I'm your mother. Trout called earlier while you were resting. Sounds like I'm the only one you're upset with."

"I don't want Trout to get hurt. I couldn't bear to see him with a broken heart because—"

"Because you're overly protective, and with good reason. You two were meant to grow together. He's more than a sturdy ole wrangler— he's a guardian angel."

She was right.

"Hope you can forgive me someday. Hope you can see past the clothes and makeup, my antics, my overboard instincts that get in the way."

"You're not wearing fancy duds or makeup now. I like you best this way." I peered through the camera viewfinder and took her picture.

CHAPTER 11

I woke before dawn, still pregnant, and showered, then dressed. Tiptoeing, I stopped to listen outside Mom's bedroom. No light trickled from the seam at the bottom of the door. I peeked in to see her tucked beneath the quilted comforter, her hair fanned across the silk pillowcase she'd brought with her.

Last night she'd not been her usual self at dinner. She'd savored one glass of wine and gone to bed early. She'd said she had things to think over, which meant she stayed in her room working on clothing designs. The keyboard tapping had been unmistakable. The conversation with Hermione muffled yet recognizably business.

After eating my oatmeal with sliced banana, I turned on the coffee, set a place for my mom at the table, and left fruit and muffins on the counter before making my way outside. The cool morning darkness ensured a new day. I put my camera in the truck and drove to the barn. Dad waited for me at the pasture gate, his stance clear in meaning.

He helped me from the truck.

"Morning, Dad."

"Morning, sweetheart. Dinner was interesting last night."

"How so?"

"Your mother was awfully quiet. She didn't quite seem like herself." He took off his gloves and tucked them into his back pocket. "Is there anything you want to talk about?"

"We haven't had a clean-cut therapy session between us in a long time."

"Call it what you want, Chloe. You've got a lot on your plate."

"Wish it would've have been a hot pickle and beef sandwich this morning. The regular oatmeal and banana isn't cutting it. What do overdue mommas eat to move things along? Something spicy? Cupcakes? I read celebrities eat something called a maternity salad. Wonder where I could find one of those."

"Talking in circles won't solve anything."

Leaning on the fence, I steepled my hands beneath my chin. "Mom and I are working through things the best we can. And by the way, she kissed Trout."

With a pinched brow, Dad groaned.

"You asked. What else do you want to know?"

"I'm not sure. Maybe I should've sent Maggie to talk to you."

"Not your style, Dad, and you know it."

We watched the sun lift the morning fog.

"Heard you haven't had any more interest in the nanny position."

"Now look who's changing the subject. And no, I haven't. Maria Santos hasn't returned my phone calls. I'm bummed—she had a lot going for her. Funny how I was hedging bets on a hunch. No one's made contact through the posts Mom made either. I want someone who's dependable."

"Are we talking about sitters or your mother?"

"Both, I guess. Mom brews like Old Faithful, but she's not as predictable. I'd like to figure her out."

"Maybe it's not your job to figure her out."

"Sure would help though."

"At the risk of being voted off the island, I'd say you've spent your time borrowing trouble and keeping your distance. One of these days, your mother might surprise you. I suppose surprise all of us. She hasn't come to me with any crazy ideas, so I think we're headed in the right direction." He took the crackling radio from his belt and adjusted the volume.

"I'd say kissing Trout was a pretty big surprise." I patted my dad on the shoulder and flashed a fake toothy smile.

Tristan, Silas, Justin, and Quinn moseyed from the barn with their rides.

"That's a mighty fine brood of wranglers."

"It's that time," Dad said.

"The horses await. This *really* is my favorite time of day." In the distance, from behind the towering pines on the mountainside, the herd stepped into the morning light one by one.

"They aren't the only ones waiting, Chloe." Dad walked away and greeted the crew.

DAD AND I had made a trip into town to Lou's Hardware. The quiet drive along the river gave me a reprieve from the house. Giving Mom space seemed like the right thing to do. Dad enjoyed the change of scenery as much as I did, and if I went into labor, he'd know what to do.

"Thanks, Dad. I needed an outing." I unbuckled my seat belt.

"Yeah, sometimes a trip to Lou's cleanses the soul. Nothing like the smell of paint thinner, fertilizer, and drain solvent." His eyes sparkled.

We laughed and got out of the truck. Glad and Lola waited for us in the yard. Glad handed her radio to Dad. Lola paced with an uneasy gait.

"Quinn wants to speak to you," Glad said.

"Hey, Quinn. Chloe and I are back."

"Silas and I have our hands full with a dozen or so who found their way to the bend in the river in the north pasture near the far border. They're spooked and running every which way. Got calves in the water. Was wondering if you could lend a hand."

Matt broke into the conversation. "Maggie and I are on our way."

"If I could get on a horse, I'd beat you all there," I said. The gnawing impulse to spring into action was alive as ever.

"Drop me off at the barn and meet me out there, Chloe." Dad handed me the key to his truck.

Even with the running board, I struggled to get into the driver's seat. I stopped Glad before she could say anything. "I got this. Babies or no babies, I'm getting into this truck. We've got work to do."

"Go get 'em, cowgirl." She threw her hands in the air. "Wait. Lola and I are coming too."

"Ida May would be proud of you," Dad said, getting into the passenger's seat. "Nothing slowed her down either. It was her way or the highway."

"She's riding on my shoulder, Dad. I was born

to be foreman." I waited for Glad to get settled in the back seat, put the truck into drive, and headed for the barn.

"Trout did a mighty fine job of training you. Starting young was a great idea."

"Sneaky," I said with a smile.

After I parked, Dad got out, mounted Breeze, who was tied to the hitching post in the shade, and headed out. Glad got into the front seat and buckled up. The truck left a dusty cloud behind us as I drove toward the main road. At the bridge just beyond the 617 sign, Mom waved me down. She wore running gear and neon orange running shoes. Her brow glistened with sweat.

"You weren't here when Dad and I drove in a few minutes ago."

"Just got here." Mom pointed to the trail parallel to the river. "I came from over there. I've got to get my exercise somehow, since there's no gym." She showed me the watch on her wrist that tracked distance and was synced with her phone.

"Glad and I are going to help with the cattle. Do you want to come?"

"I'll see you when you get back."

"Come on. We won't be long. There'll be wranglers on horses and cows in the river."

"I'd like to get this last mile in."

"Suit yourself. But you haven't lived until you've seen a cowboy work the cattle free from the river."

"Be careful." Mom rested her hand on the open window. "I'll see the pasture another day."

Glad and I watched her jog to the trailhead. Lola stuck her snout out the window and barked.

"I wish she'd just come with us," I said to Glad.

"She's missing all the fun." Glad shook her head.

Mom glanced over her shoulder at us, then turned around, called my name through cupped hands, and jogged back to the truck.

"I've changed my mind. I'm coming with you." She untied the windbreaker from around her waist and slipped into it.

"Hop in, buttercup, the cows are on the run," Glad said, pulling the brim of her hat tight against her brow.

The radio beeped, and I parked at the end of the drive to answer the call. No one replied to my response. I shook the radio. The static feedback blared. I adjusted the volume, and Matt's voice cut in and out.

"Maggie, Matt, Dad, anyone, can you hear me?" Dad answered, then the airway went dead.

"Something's wrong."

Glad rolled down her window. The breeze caught the loose strands of hair framing her face. I glanced at Mom in the rearview mirror. Lola whined. I checked and double-checked for oncoming traffic, then accelerated. Glad and I jerked back.

"Maybe you should let me drive," Glad said.

A brisk burst of wind blew dust across the road, making it difficult to see.

"Or I can drive," Mom said. "Did you know your camera is on the seat back here? Looks like Lola drooled on it."

"I'm fine. I'll wipe the drool off," I replied.

"You're in no condition to drive," Glad bantered. "And I *can* touch the pedals."

"Pregnant women drive all the time." I gripped the steering wheel tighter as the front tires dipped in a chuckhole.

"It's not that. You're upset, and that's when accidents happen. Your head's not thinking about driving. It's thinking about getting there," Mom said.

The river's swift current bubbled over the rocky riverbed the road paralleled. Its easy-flowing appearance could be misleading. "The river may be pretty, but it can be dangerous. You never know when you'll lose your footing or step into an unexpected swell." I eased up on the gas as I navigated the bend in the road.

"Sounds like you're talking about more than the river," Glad said.

"I agree," Mom added.

"I appreciate the concern, ladies, but I've got this. We're almost there." I drove to the cut-in leading to the pasture. In the distance, Maggie rode Cora, her red roan, along the riverbank with a rope in hand. "What *is* going on?"

"I don't think there's a road here," Glad said.

"There doesn't need to be one. If anyone knows that, it's you, Gladiola. I've done this before." Lola's ears went back; she fixated on the scene ahead. Her front legs trembled as we got closer. Faint whimpers escaped her jowls between yips.

Glad white-knuckled the armrest between us. When I realized 313 was stuck in the river, I parked the truck, opened the door, and slid out of the seat. Lola jumped down and ran ahead. Poor 311 stood close by with her head hung low, unwilling to move without 313. Her bellows curdled the air.

Glad and Mom watched from the truck.

Dad on Breeze shouted orders. Maggie spoke to

her horse in a gentle voice, but Cora's reluctance to follow directions was obvious as she sidestepped along the riverbank. Dad also shouted multiple times at Matt, who was knee-deep in water, rubbing the back of his head. Slapping his thigh, he finally stepped away from the calf and clenched his fist. Walking away wasn't in his nature, especially when cattle were involved.

Dad lassoed 313 then gave Breeze a swift kick. Maggie followed his orders and beckoned Cora to move in the same direction. I rested my hand on Matt's shoulder.

"Your dad got here just in time," he said.

"What happened?" A wicked shiver drifted through my veins.

"I'll tell you later."

"I want to know now. Where's your hat?" The shrill tone of my voice surprised me.

"Downriver." Matt winced and held the back of his head. Blood oozed through his damp hair, a warning in his stare.

I watched Dad and Maggie cradle 313 between them, coaxing her like a scared child.

"I can't, and I won't stand down. As long as my legs work, I'm going in!" Matt stepped into the river, determined to finish what he had started, despite my father's orders.

Feeling helpless, I watched from the sidelines.

Muffled thuds of cantering grew louder. Quinn and Tristan rode like fury across the field, Gypsy's high stride swift and purposeful. Quinn crouched low on his spotted quarter horse, Chaplin. They came to an abrupt halt and dismounted with flying leaps. Tristan grabbed Matt by the shoulder. The men exchanged silent glances. With a nod, Matt and Tristan waded farther into the water. Matt steadied himself on Maggie's rope until he found his footing.

Glad got out of the truck and held my hand. I ached to be useful. This was the kind of drama I knew how to handle. I glanced back at my mom, who was talking into her watch before approaching with the camera I had in the truck.

Dad ordered Matt to hang onto the rope and not let go regardless of what the calf did. Tristan crouched at 313's hind end. Matt was drenched from head to toe, his shirt collar stained with blood.

Mom stood beside me. She focused the camera lens and snapped photos. Before I knew it, she was on the riverbank, a stone's throw from the calves.

"Mom. No. Give them their space! It's not safe." Before I could take a step, Glad pulled me backward. "She's gonna get herself or someone else hurt."

"Get back, Brook!" Glad yelled, dropped my hand, and went after my mom. Glad lost her balance on the uneven ground and fell to her knees.

Maggie yelped louder than the chaos. Dad barked orders. His voice boomed.

"Glad!" I hurried to help her up. "Stay here."

"One more time. Chloe's got Gladiola," Dad called out, giving Maggie a nod. Maggie followed his lead. She sat tall and sure as any wrangler in the saddle.

Matt pulled on the rope. The strain was evident in everyone's pinched stares. Tristan and Quinn braced themselves against 313's hindquarters while Dad lassoed her with a second rope. On the count of three, he pulled and Tristan and Quinn pushed.

Mom crouched low and waved Quinn off when he left Tristan's side to escort her to a safer vantage point. His scowl was one I'd never seen before, his face flushed, his expression beyond angry.

The tension drained from Matt's face as the calf pawed at the muddy bank to gain her footing. Glad squeezed my hand, her gold wedding band hard against my skin. Her love for her husband, Walter James, remained constant even if he had been gone almost more years than I'd been alive.

Matt stumbled onto dry ground, sat down, and avoided my gaze. Dad and Maggie dismounted their rides to finish the job. Their jeans were soiled and soaked. Mom continued taking pictures.

Dad knelt, inspecting Matt's head. I watched on.

"What happened?" I could barely speak. Pressure built behind my eyes.

"When we got here, Matt was in the water." Dad held a bandanna against the gash in Matt's head.

"I was more than in the water. Just tell her. She'll badger me until she hears the whole story." Matt slumped forward.

Dad knocked his hat back. "Maybe you should tell her yourself, son."

"I was under the water. I went in before your dad got here. The toe of my boot got caught under a rock. I fell backward trying to catch myself and cracked my head. I was facedown, and Maggie couldn't get to me."

"You're going to need a handful of stitches. Chloe will keep an eye on you tonight. If you feel sick, dizzy, anything out of the ordinary, we'll call Doc Payne. I'll give him a head's up. Tristan will take the calves back to the ranch. They're going into the pen closest to Chloe's house," Dad said. "And they'll stay there."

"I'm guessing you'll stitch up my head."

"Unless you want to call Doc Payne now."

"I'd rather not."

Gypsy strolled over and sniffed Matt. Her whiskers brushed his cheek, and Matt patted her nose.

"That isn't a horse who's holding a grudge," I said. "You're going back in the truck with me. Dad will take your horse."

"I'm sorry," Matt said.

"For what?" Dad scratched his temple.

"I should've waited until everyone was here."

Maggie handed Matt her neckerchief. "Hold this clean one on the back of your head."

"You did what you thought was right. Sometimes, waiting causes more problems," Dad said, helping Matt to his feet.

"I couldn't let anything happen to your cows." A dark shadow drifted across Matt's gaze, his jawline rigid.

"You really should see the doctor." I inspected his face and neck for additional injuries.

Dad cupped his hands below Maggie's stirrup. She was back up on Cora and ready to ride home. Mom stood on the sidelines talking into her watch.

She called to my dad, but he waved her off.

"Not now, Brook. Get in the truck and go back to the ranch."

Tristan pulled two halters from Gypsy's saddlebags while 313 meandered in the opposite direction. Then 311 nudged him as if to say it was 313's idea to play in the water. Tristan let her sniff the leather halter. "Sorry, girl. We don't need any more casualties today." He placed the halter over her head, his deep voice lulling her into compliance. He led her closer to Gypsy, who had sought out a patch of sweetgrass. Calf 313 followed suit when she realized 311 was headed elsewhere.

"Chloe, no wild driving. Can you handle Glad, Matt, and *your mother*?" Dad's serious stare was not to be tested.

"Not a problem." I took Mom by the arm and lowered my voice. "What were you thinking? You could've gotten hurt. Or worse. You jeopardized everyone's safety. Glad fell because of you. But you wouldn't know because you were too busy taking pictures. And when a wrangler gives you his hand, you take it."

Mom handed me the camera, and I turned it off. She stood speechless, and she was never speechless.

Maggie rode toward us, and Glad waved to her.

"Mom, are you okay?"

"I'm fine." Glad brushed off the knees of her jeans. "I'll see you back at the house." She beamed with pride, taking in the sight of Maggie riding away, swift and tall.

My heart pinched at the exchange. "Come on, Gladiola, let's get this cowboy home." I sounded sadder than a calf who'd lost its momma.

With my hand on Matt's forearm, Glad, Mom, and I walked him back to the truck.

"I can ride my horse." Matt took the bandanna from the back of his head and handed it to me.

"Get in the truck," Glad said. "You're done riding today, cowboy. My old soul can't handle much more."

Matt's chest rose and fell with a shudder. He closed his eyes and swallowed his dented pride. "I'll sit in the bed." He released the tailgate and invited Lola to ride along. She nuzzled up to him and licked his face.

"You sure you don't want to ride in the cab?"

Glad touched my hand, her silent stare more intense than a stern lecture. Matt glanced up, his gaze laced with what I thought was embarrassment and disappointment. I bit my bottom lip, got in the driver's seat, turned the key in the ignition, and glanced in the rearview mirror at my mother in the back seat.

I drove across the bumpy terrain carefully, not wanting to jostle my precious cargo.

"He could've drowned," I said to Glad, my eyes focused on the distant mountains. Their jagged peaks stabbed the blue sky. I glanced in the rearview mirror again. Mom stared out the window, her bottom lip quivered.

DAD SUTURED MATT'S head, and I paced. The scene in Dad's office was like an old Western: Dad with his leather medical bag and reading glasses balanced at the end of his nose, Matt with a glass of whiskey and a sore disposition.

Maggie poked her head into the room. "I called Doc Payne. He wants to see Matt."

Matt slugged down the last swallow of whiskey. "Who's driving me?"

Before I could answer, Dad said he would.

"There'll be food waiting when you get home," Maggie said.

Dad secured the last suture, organized his medical bag, and told Matt to meet him at the truck. The weight of defeat settled firmly in his shoulders.

"You didn't do anything wrong. Accidents happen," I said.

"I know, but I should've waited for the guys. I shouldn't have put Maggie in that position. Silas is off, and I knew the calf was in trouble. I owe your dad a big one."

"I'm impulsive all the time. I get it. I'm thankful you're okay. Quit being so hard on yourself."

"I expect better," he said.

I walked with Matt and Dad out to Dad's truck. Mom stood beneath a shade tree in the yard, talking on her phone. She ended the call and joined us.

"Are you going to be okay?" she asked Matt.

"Yeah. Thanks for asking." He got in the truck and shut the door.

We watched them drive away. When the dust cleared, Mom looked at me.

"Where'd you put your camera, Chloe?"

"Why?"

"I'd like to delete the photos I took. You don't need any reminders of what happened here today."

"I already took care of it. I can't believe you took pictures of everything. The people. Matt, his injury. His bloody shirt. That's not okay. Just because they're deleted doesn't mean it didn't happen. I don't think I need to say any more. If you'll excuse me, I'm needed in the barn. We could use some extra help."

Mom took off her watch and left it on the porch with her phone. "I'm coming with you."

CHAPTER 12

DINNER WAS QUIET, and we had all agreed to skip the nightly bonfire. I'd gotten ready for bed when the sun went down, finished reading the book of poetry Silas had loaned me, and went downstairs for ginger ale to settle my stomach. Mom sat at the kitchen table with her laptop and sketchbook. She wore a chic pair of tortoiseshell eyeglasses, her hair swept up in a messy chignon.

"I like your specs," I said.

"Cheaters. My eyes aren't what they used to be. There's a place back home that restores vintage frames and fits them with custom lenses."

"How's the collection coming?" I sat across from her and sipped my soda.

"We're ahead of schedule at the moment. Hermione's working on marketing with our team, and I'm brainstorming future themes. I've got so many ideas."

"That's good. I'm sure you two will achieve many great things." I fiddled with the fabric swatches Mom had grouped by color next to her computer. "We should talk about what happened out there today. So much went wrong and could've been worse. I've been thinking about it all evening." When I thought about the photos she'd taken and I'd deleted, my stomach turned over.

"I've been thinking, too. I got in the way."

"It's more than getting in the way, Mom. People's lives were at stake. The cattle, too. That was more than business out there. This is my life."

"I thought Matt was staying with us tonight," Mom said.

"Me too. He decided to stay with Trout. Thought he'd be interrupting our mother-daughter time."

"He's quite thoughtful, Chloe. Intelligent, too. He had a scary afternoon."

"And all I could do was watch." I took a cherry antacid from the bottle on the table and chewed it.

"You can't prevent every accident. It's not possible."

"I have to try, Mom. Matt's not just staying with Trout to give us our space. More than the accident upset him. He's not here because of you. I thought it best to be honest." I raked my fingers through my hair.

"Oh, Chloe—"

"I'm not sure where we go from here. First Trout. Now this. Trout's made himself scarce and now Matt. Again, I'm watching from the sidelines of my own life. You'll finish your visit, go back home, and I'll be left behind to pick up the pieces." I finished my ginger ale.

"When you were little, you consoled your father, too. Your sense of responsibility is larger-than-life. I wish I had an iota of your strength." Her words were nothing more than a whisper. "You're right. You'll be left with the aftermath. I never meant to cross the line with Trout. And—today. I'm sorry about Matt and *your* Gladiola."

"She's everyone's Gladiola, especially Maggie's. Can you imagine how heartbroken Maggie would be if something happened to her mom?"

Mom closed her laptop and laced her fingers together. "On the brighter side, I only had one glass of wine with dinner." She held up the empty tumbler and shook the ice. "Came home and went straight for the sparkling H2O. You're out of limes. Thought you'd want to know." She went to the cupboard, found a wineglass, and poured herself some Chardonnay. "I hope you don't mind."

"Seriously, Mom? I don't have the energy for this. You're a grown woman. Old enough to make considerate decisions without my two cents."

"You were remarkable with the horses in the barn today. Trout's not the only one you have wrapped around your little finger."

"No one's wrapped around my little finger, not even Trout. It's called respect."

I shook the bottle of rainbow-colored antacids, found another cherry-flavored one, and chewed it. Mom stood at the counter and sipped her wine. I flipped through the pages of her sketchbook.

"My nerves get the best of me. It's too quiet sometimes. Like now. I don't like the quiet. Watching you all work this afternoon took those nerves away. Would be great television."

"Are you listening to yourself?" I lowered my tone.

"Today, when I was jogging, I found myself lost in the landscape. Social gatherings and networking didn't matter. The next collection didn't matter. The mentor program didn't matter. Nothing mattered. All that mattered was being here. When you invited me to see the cattle and I walked away from a disappointed daughter, all that mattered was being with you."

"It *is* magical, excitement and all. But, Mom, this isn't a fairy tale you've stepped into. There's no magic wand or pixie dust to rewind time. If I had any of those things, I'd erase this afternoon. The fact that you—" I drummed my fingertips on the table. There was no sense in starting a senseless debate.

"It's time for bed." Mom hesitated to leave. A hint of speculation lit her gaze. "Tomorrow's a new day."

"I'll be up in a few minutes," I said.

After Mom went upstairs, I opened her sketchbook to the back and colored in sky blue teardrops until the blank page was filled. I straightened the colored pencils and closed the book.

Mom returned, her footsteps soft against the wood floor. She'd changed into yoga pants and a tank top. Loose ringlets rained down over her shoulders.

"I forgot to say good night," she said.

"Night, Mom."

"Chloe—"

"Yes, Mom."

"For what it's worth, I'm sorry about today. I'll make sure to apologize to everyone tomorrow."

"I'm sure they'd appreciate it. Thanks, Mom."

"And I heard what you said. Maggie would be devastated. I should've answered you. I really am glad everyone is all right." She padded away.

I loaded the dishwasher, turned off the lights,

and made my way upstairs. A wispy breeze swept in through the open window at the end of the hall. Grandma's lace curtains I couldn't bear to part with billowed in the dim light. I'd taken them down when the walls had been refinished, and as much as I thought I should make this place mine, those curtains found their way back up. They spoke to me, said that my inherited home would never truly be my own, for it was built from the blood, sweat, tears, and love of those who came before me. My foundation existed long before I was born.

I got into my cozy sleigh bed, rested against the curved headboard, and took Trout's chapter book for youngsters from the nightstand. The lamp was no brighter than the moonlight drifting through the window. The note tucked between the pages, that I'd seen at Trout's house, fell onto my belly. I held it closer to the bulb to read it.

My circle begins and ends with you.

I fingered the tattered edges of the paper. Memories of Frankie, the broken crow from my childhood, flitted to the forefront of my mind. I'd found him injured, taken him in, and befriended him. When he'd flown away without saying goodbye, I cried, and Trout consoled me, told me Frankie had to fly in his own time, not mine.

So did my mother.

I read the first page of the story Trout had read as a boy, closed my eyes, and imagined Frankie catching the tail end of the north wind for the ride of his life.

"Chloe."

I opened my eyes. Mom stood at the edge of my bed, still in yoga pants and a tank top, her thin arms accentuated by her fitting workout regime. She ran her fingers through her hair and tied it back with an elastic band. With the day behind us and the blanket of night upon us, we were *just* two people; we were mother and daughter. She sat on my bed where Maggie usually sat when we shared advice or girl talk when I'd lived in the main house.

"Last fall, I thought I lost the baby. I had no idea I was carrying twins at that point. I was riding on the ridge, and a bobcat chased my horse. Lola was injured, and I went to the hospital. When the doctor told me I could lose the baby, I felt a shift inside me I can't explain. I knew—I was meant to be a mother." I took a deep breath. "Why do you work so hard?"

"My therapist asks me the same question." Mom stroked the hem of the sheet. "Working drowns out the things I don't want to deal with, mostly spending time by myself. Like you, I don't know what to do with me at times either. Work pushes regret to the background. I've spent my life making a name for myself, and I don't know how to do anything else."

Mom inspected the tattered paper belonging to Trout. She handed it back to me with a half smile on her lips. I used it to mark the place where I had left off reading.

I swallowed the knot at the back of my throat. "Matt has never met his mother. He was adopted. Left on a doorstep. We've talked about moms a lot." I held my mother's stare. "You're not the only one who feels the power of silence. For me, silence happens when we're together. It's like being in a dream. I yell to you, and you just can't hear me."

I took my tattered purple journal from the nightstand drawer and handed it to her. She flipped through the pages, touching each picture as if she were reliving the moments of her life that I'd cut from magazines and taped into a notebook. "People say and do foolish things when they're hurting." I scrunched up the edge of the downy comforter between my fingers. "What was your mother like?"

"My mother and I fought. We cut ties when I

left for LA. While I was busy making something of myself, my mother became ill. I didn't know she had ovarian cancer until after she'd passed away. Her lawyer called to tell me, and I was so angry. After three years with Dr. Clifton, my therapist, I now know that I was angry because we let our differences define our relationship. When I peeled away the resentment, I discovered I didn't hate her. I wanted her to see me. I wanted her to understand my dream was different from hers. I wanted her to accept me for who I was and not what she wanted me to be.

"Our arguments obliterated the good times, and we grew apart. Instead of straightening each other's crowns, we knocked them off. Determined, I did my thing without her. When she passed, her estate was settled and she was buried within a week. I wish it would've ended differently." She took a deep breath. "More?"

I nodded.

"I thought clout was important. I wanted her to see that I was worthy of more than the life she wanted me to have. I'm sorry I robbed you of knowing her. I'm sorry I robbed myself. I hope our story has a better ending." She smoothed out the sheet. "More?"

"Yes," I whispered.

"Watching you take after your father as you grew older made me feel less relevant. Then Maggie came along, and you loved her so much. It hurt, Chloe. She was everything you wanted, and I couldn't compete with that. But I did know how to work and be successful, so I worked harder. You were always your father's Paris girl."

"He says that, too."

"I can't believe you still have the necklace I gave you when Maggie brought you to Chicago to see me. The shoot was at the Bean. Do you remember being doted on and dressing up? I still have the photos."

"I do remember. I have the photos, too. I wear this necklace almost every day. I still have the baby blue box it came in." I undid the clasp and set my necklace with the silver heart charm on the nightstand. "I take it off when I sleep and shower."

"If I remember correctly, once Maggie and I got past the butterflies of being together, we had a good time." Mom touched the charm, bit her bottom lip, then put her hand back in her lap.

"We had a great time. That day at your photo shoot was one of the best days of my life." I leafed through the journal. "When I was in elementary school, the other kids didn't think you existed.

They thought I lied about you being my mother, because we looked so different and you were never around."

I took the neatly folded, raggedy photograph tucked near the back of the book. Mom's face creased, and the ink faded. "Do you know why this picture looks like this?" I searched her gaze. "I carried this in my pocket for two years to keep you close."

Mom left the room and returned with the *La Chic* magazine with her spread, a pen, and her sketchbook. She crawled under the covers next to me, and I let her. Her shiny manicured lavender toes matched her shiny manicured lavender fingernails. She opened the magazine and un-capped the marker.

"See this blouse. These embroidered blue trian-gles are the mountains that protect the valley where Winston's cattle graze. The yellow dots symbolize your light. The white organic shapes that look like clouds are the cattle. Each color, each shape in these designs tell your story. Those aren't just stripes on the hatband. Blue represents water, orange represents the sun, and they're equal in proportion because the earth needs balance. The thin umber lines uniting the complimentary colors represent the soil."

"I ordered the hat," I said.

"Smart girl. It's a forever piece."

"I kept those photos because I'm proud of you. To remember you when the gap between us was so big I thought I would forget you. Because you're important to me, Mom."

"I know," she whispered.

"I want to learn from both our mistakes. Not just for me but for my children."

"Me too. I could talk about fashion all night, but you should get some sleep. It's been a long day. I appreciate your candidness." She got up and tucked in the sheet.

"Good night, Coco."

"Good night, Paris girl."

CHAPTER 13

GETTING COMFORTABLE FOR a good night's sleep was impossible, and the conversation with my mother steeped a late-night buzz I couldn't shake. I switched on the lamp and opened the storybook to the page where I'd last left off, marked by the scrap of paper. I devoured the text while popping the allotted amount of fruit-flavored anti-acids. About halfway through the book, I closed my eyes and thought about the boy who'd been gifted a book and made friends with a horse. Finally, content, I fell asleep around four a.m. knowing I'd miss Dad and the wranglers run the horses.

I pushed away the tickle on my cheek.

"Wake up, Chloe." Matt stroked my hair.

"What time is it?" I rubbed my eyes.

"It's ten o'clock. Your mom called. She wanted you to sleep, but thought I should check in. Said you had a late night."

"We did. I couldn't sleep. Where's my book?"

"It's here. I marked your place with the scrap

of paper you had in your hand."

I propped myself up. "How's your head?"

"It's fine. Trout took good care of me. How about breakfast? Hot pickle and beef sandwich or oatmeal? Take your pick."

"Can I have both?"

"The combination sounds savage, but it's your world. I'll be back in a bit."

Matt left the room and spoke to my mother in the hallway. Matt thanked her for calling him, then went downstairs. I swung my legs over the side of the bed, then shuffled to the bathroom. I brushed my hair back and secured it with an elastic band, splashed cool water on my face, and patted it dry with a fresh towel.

When I came out of the bathroom, I leaned against the doorjamb of the babies' room, warding off the pain in my lower back. Sitting in bed hadn't done wonders for my already-aching body. Sometime between yesterday and today, someone had snuck two life-sized stuffed ponies in the nursery.

"Too much?" Matt stood on the landing with a tray of food and a sly grin.

"You did this?"

"Yes, ma'am. Kid friendly. Coco approved."

"Oh brother." The aroma of pickles and beef

tickled my nose. My backache quickly turned into a contraction I couldn't ignore. I leaned into the wall.

"Chloe!" Matt's eyes were big as could be. He juggled the tray before setting it on the floor.

My knees went weak, and I bit my lip.

"Do we need to go to the hospital?"

I hesitated to answer him. "As much as I'd like to get these babies out of me, I don't think so. I'm not feeling the urge."

"If you're in labor, we have a drive. This isn't something you can put off until the timing suits you." He noted the time.

"I don't know if I'm in labor. I've never done this before. And if I have anything to say about it, I won't be doing this again. It's cutting into my horse time, not to mention other things." I stared at him. "Tell me anything to get my mind off the pain."

"Let's get you off your feet."

"Now there's an idea I can get on board with. Breakfast awaits." I grabbed his hand. "I'm good."

"You sure?"

"I'm fine." I pushed my shoulders back, and a rush of water covered my feet. "Uh-oh. Mom was right when she said nothing good can come from kissing a cowboy."

Mom poked her head out of her room. "Did I hear I was right about something?" She rushed into the hallway and stopped short when she noticed the pool of wetness. "We have to get you to the hospital."

"I'll get the duffel. We'll call Maggie and your dad before we leave." Matt disappeared into the bedroom.

"Make sure to wrap up that sandwich. I'm taking it with me." I kicked off my slippers. "Is someone going to clean this up?"

Matt poked his head into the hallway.

"That's what you're worried about?" he and Mom said in unison.

"When I get home, I don't want this puddle to be here. I just had the floors done."

Matt tripped over himself before disappearing back into the bedroom. Mom fiddled with the bandanna on my head, her blue gaze more intense than ever.

"What?" I asked.

"I didn't notice the embroidered initials in the design before."

I patted my head, remembering which bandanna I had on. "This one belonged to Ida May. She embroidered her initials on her scarves and Grandpa's initials on *his* scarves because she thought Grandpa hoarded them."

"Ahhh," she said.

"But we can talk more about that later. My sleeping pants are soaked. I'm standing in a pool"—I glanced down and waved my hands around, sputtering about the mess—"of amniotic fluid, and you're worried about what I'm wearing. How about I change into clean clothes, then we'll worry about my accessories. Better yet, design bandannas you'd approve of, and I'll buy them all. I like embroidery, paisley, and flowers. Maybe Hermione could design some using her Native American roots. I'd definitely buy those, too. But you should know, I won't give away the ones that belonged to Ida May and Winston."

"Who's the diva now? Quit chattering and change your clothes. I'll call Maggie." Mom shooed me away, then wiped up the floor after Matt tossed her a towel.

I followed Matt into the bedroom and took a bite of my sandwich. "Did you know accessories can divide a household? Can you help me with these pants?" I wiggled out of my pajama bottoms, then my granny panties, hoping not to see them for a long while.

Matt tossed a pair of clean underwear on the bed and turned his back to me. "What are you doing?" I asked.

"Giving you some privacy."

"You do know, privacy is going to be thrown out the window when I hike my feet into those stirrups at the hospital?"

"Come on, Chloe, we need to go. I want to get you to the hospital *before* the babies come."

He handed me a pair of sweatpants.

"Not these. The stretchy jeans."

Matt dropped the sweats on the floor and rifled through the denim pile heaped on the chair.

"Third pair down."

"Geez, Chloe. This is crazy."

I sat on the bed and wiggled into them, the elastic snug against my waist. "Boots, please."

He handed me my favorite pair worn almost clean through at the toe. "Not those. The studded pair."

"Really?"

"Please!"

Mom knocked at the door.

"Hold on a second," I called.

"Chloe. Hurry up, we need to get moving." Matt put the boots on my feet.

"Mom and I had a nitty-gritty conversation last night. Please don't take this away from me. Besides, I'm not wearing a shirt." I grabbed a flannel button-down from the closet and put it on.

"What exactly happened between you two?" Matt raised his brow.

"I'll tell you in the truck." I slid the bandanna from my head. "Put this in the bag. I'll want it later. Make sure I have my pajamas. Oh, and that sandwich and my new underwear, and stop looking so worried. You've been the no-nonsense one. I need that now. Panicky Matt isn't invited to this rodeo." I pointed to my white cowboy hat on the hook near the closet. "Can you please hand that to me?" I pulled the elastic tie from my ponytail and fluffed my hair.

"Chloe—let's go. You never know when those babies will come." Matt checked the duffel and slung it over his thick cowboy shoulder.

Mom knocked at the door again.

"Is she coming with us?" he mouthed.

"I don't know. We didn't talk about it." He handed me the hat. I put it on, then stood—kind of. The next pain radiated across my back and into my belly. "How do I look?" I asked through pinched lips.

"As always, beautiful, sass and all." He kissed my cheek. "You ready?"

"As ready as I'll ever be."

Mom knocked again. Her shrill request to hurry sounded frantic. I opened the door. Mom slung her purse over her shoulder, her jaw taut. She straightened my hat and smiled.

"That's more like it," she said.

She combed the ends of my hair with her fingers, then pointed to the clean floor.

"Can we go now?" Matt asked.

"Yes," Mom and I said in unison.

CHAPTER 14

BEFORE MATT COULD check me in at the hospital's reception desk, an attendant with a stethoscope hanging around his neck whisked me away to a room. I stripped and put on the drafty gown lying on the bed.

"Come in," I answered the knock at the door. Mom entered and straightened my gown. In that moment, she wasn't the blonde bombshell workaholic with an accolade of achievements and annoying quirks. She was my mother, plain and simple. She bore an invisible cloak of scars like the rest of us. I lowered my chin, biting my quivering lip.

"You would think they'd have nicer gowns. Maybe a plush spa robe?" I pulled at the cotton sheath, trying to cover my bare areas.

"You really are my daughter," she said.

"Yes, I am."

"Well"—she tugged at the hem of her blouse and squared her shoulders—"that's good to know. I should design hospital gowns for expecting mothers, with an inspirational message in the pocket. Fortune cookie wisdom in a terrycloth hug. I'll get on it." She straightened the dresser and smoothed down the bed. "I can't believe my baby is having babies."

"Will you come in if I need you?"

"You know I will." She rubbed my belly. "Coco will meet you soon," she said to the babies.

A wave of emotion slipped through my giggle, and Mom wiped my cheeks dry. I wiggled into bed and blew loose hair from my face.

Matt came in and set my duffel in the lounger near the window. Mom took the ice chips from the nurse who followed on his heels. The nurse plugged in another monitor and checked the flowing mass of tubes.

"Do you need anything, Chloe?" Matt asked.

"A body double." I squeezed his hand as the next contraction came.

"I don't think that's possible," Mom said. "How about acupuncture? I'm sure there's someone here who can help with that." She waited for an answer. "By the look on your faces, that's not an option. If you change your mind, let me know." She dialed her phone and left a message for a Dr. Linden to remain on standby. "Dr. Linden is a personal friend. He swears acupuncture relieves labor pains."

"Mom—"

She patted Matt on the shoulder. "I'm sorry about getting in the way yesterday. I should've known better. It won't happen again. Sometimes, I can't help myself. Like now. How's your head feeling?" She fanned her cheeks. "My daughter's having babies. There really should be a physician in here. A glass of red wine sure would be nice." She took a cleansing breath and massaged her temples.

"My head is fine. Thanks for asking," Matt replied. His gaze met mine.

"You're on your own." I white-knuckled the bedrail, then whispered to the twins, "If you ever have babies, I'll do my best to behave. I promise."

"You take care of my daughter, cowboy. That gash on the back of your head is nothing compared to what she's about to go through."

"Yes, ma'am."

"If my daughter can take time to coordinate an outfit for the hospital, I can be a ma'am occasionally. Remember that when I'm having a cocktail. I won't care as much."

"Duly noted. I'll take good care of your daughter, Coco."

"You'll both do fine. Coco will be in the waiting room." Mom smiled. "I probably shouldn't refer to myself in the third person."

"Boy, is she wound up. Good luck to the nurses at the nurses' station." I plucked ice chips from the foam cup. "They should make these things out of whiskey, maybe a nice smooth scotch." I took a deep breath. "I told you we didn't need to hurry. I could still be at home in bed. I should've eaten more of that sandwich. I could've slept through this. The babies will spend their lives making me wait or rush to catch up."

"Stop yammering. You're here, and this is happening. Yes, the babies will do things in their own time, and you couldn't have slept through this."

"Don't underestimate me, cowboy."

"My mistake." He put a chunk of ice in his mouth. "Yeah, whiskey would be a great idea."

The nurse came in and checked my vitals.

"The doctor will be in soon. You're doing great," she said.

"Is Maggie coming? And Glad?"

"Your momma is handful enough right now. I'm surprised you didn't rope Bradley into flying in."

"He wasn't available. He and his girlfriend, Red, had other plans. He said something about her uncle. All I know right now is—" I moaned and clenched my toes against the bed as the radiating pain intensified.

"Breathe, Chloe."

"Call my dad, please"—I panted—"but don't leave me in here alone." Matt smoothed my hair back. "Do I really look like a grunge rocker when I wear my bandanna?"

"Not at all. I liked your idea about your mom designing scarves."

"Good answer." I grabbed his hand. "Will you send my mom in? But when the time comes for the babies to be born, it'll be you and me. No family spectators or videos."

"I'll pinky swear to that, Momma."

"These babies better be bigger than peanuts because I want to take them home. Everything is all set up, and home cooking beats hospital food any day. I really should've eaten all of that sandwich on the way here, and those art prints on the wall are not good."

"You're exhausting." Matt ran his hand through his hair, careful not to touch his stitches.

"If you think I'm a handful, wait until the babies come. There'll be three of us. Put that in your fancy cowboy hat."

I squeezed the bed rail as the next contraction came and went. Sweat dripped from my temples.

"I can't believe you did this to me."

Matt kissed my forehead. "It was a great day though, wasn't it?" The dimple in his left cheek appeared.

"Yes, it was. Thanks for being here, cowboy."

"I've got your back. Always."

The nurse came in, greeted me cheerfully, and held my wrist to check my pulse. When the contraction subsided, I fell back against the pillows.

"I'm *really* going to call your dad now." Matt stroked my forehead. "You've got this."

"Okay, cowboy. Bet I'll be Hollywood gorgeous after delivering these babies."

"On that note, I'm leaving. I'll be back."

Mom came in and patted me down with a cool washcloth. I started to laugh.

"What's so funny, Chloe?"

"My children are going to have a Coco who believes Rodeo Drive is a god and spray tans, false eyelashes, and dreams can be achieved by making a phone call."

"Hey"—she leaned in—"someone's gotta teach them about the outside world. And the phone calls are many."

"I'm glad you're here, Mom."

"Me too. I think we're getting better about

talking through our issues."

I nodded. "Are you glad you had me?" I didn't know what made me ask.

"Absolutely, Chloe Jean." Mom pried my white knuckles from the bed frame and held my hand. Her gaze lit the room as if she were strutting the catwalk at a glitzy shoot.

"Squeeze my fingers. I swear I won't break—or pass gas."

We laughed, and she fed me ice chips.

"These don't help," I said.

"I know. I can call Dr. Linden. You ready to try the acupuncture?"

"No." I sat up. "Another shot of those pain meds would be appreciated."

"I had more than my share when I was in your position. You were no easy delivery, and your dad"—she waved her free hand—"micromanaged the nurses through the whole thing. They'd become so disgusted with him, they sent him on a wild goose chase for a pretend phone call to give me a break."

"Really? He was that bad? Here comes another contraction." Mom's thin fingers crumpled in my grip.

"Squeeze away, baby girl. Breathe." Mom's eyes brimmed with tears, and she kissed my hand.

"For the love of the sweet Lord, where is Dr. Hennessey? I want these babies out of me now." I took a deep breath and exhaled with a bellow like a momma moose protecting her calf.

A nurse I hadn't seen before came in and pulled the curtain around us. The cocoon of muted plaid was no more comforting than the faded garden prints on the wall or the ice chips.

"I'm Faith, and things are moving right along in here. Looks like we're getting close to delivery." She took my pulse and read the monitor. "You ready for more pain meds?"

I nodded and studied her fuchsia top printed with llamas wearing wildflower crowns. Her auburn hair was pulled back into a sleek ponytail.

The contractions came closer together, and the pain escalated. Matt and Dr. Hennessey appeared from behind the curtain. Dr. Hennessey's pixie bobbed as she walked the room, checking monitors and equipment. She peered through tortoiseshell glasses and checked my blood pressure.

Faith returned shortly with a syringe of medication. I lowered my head with the next contraction and stared at my mom from beneath my lashes.

"I can't wait for this part to be over," I grunted.

"If it were easy, they wouldn't call it labor. It's

time to deliver these babies. Is Mom staying?" Dr. Hennessey jotted notes in my chart.

"You and Matt need to do this together. Alone. I'll be in the waiting room. I'll let your father know what's going on."

"I'm not sure I can do this." I blinked away the pooling tears.

"You can do anything you put your mind to. It's time to muster up some of your cowgirl grit, daughter."

"Promise you won't leave, Mom." Hopefully, she would read between the lines.

"I'll be right outside the door." She left the room.

"Dr. Hennessey will make sure you're okay. Just do what she says." Matt dabbed my forehead with a fresh towel.

"Following directions is *so* not in my wheel-house, but I'll try. Thanks for not looking scared anymore," I said.

"Anything for my girls."

"Girls?" Goose bumps covered my arms. Dr. Hennessey nodded, sat on the stool, wheeled herself closer, and lifted the sheet to check my *situation*.

"I asked when I was in the hallway. I had to know. Thought it would make getting them here a

little easier for you if you knew who was coming."
Matt smiled.

"Get ready to push, Chloe," the doctor said.

"Like right now?" I grabbed at the hem of the knit blanket and twisted it with a clenched fist.

"Yes, Chloe, on the count of three. Bear down, squeeze Matt's hand, and push. I see a head."

I followed Dr. Hennessey's directions. She reported seeing the shoulders of baby number one, then ordered me to push again. Repeat pushes seemed to get us nowhere. I covered my face with my hands and groaned.

"Don't give up—we're almost there. Push! You can do it," she said.

I bore down. Images from the past flashed in my mind, from the day I met Maggie until the day I set foot on the ranch, named my first barn cat, and kissed Matt. "Can I be done now?" I moaned.

"You'll have a brief pause, then it'll be time to deliver baby girl number two."

Baby girl one was tiny and wrinkled and pink and way bigger than a peanut. My calves shook from fatigue. "I want to rest. Can someone else push baby girl number two out for me?"

"No," Dr. Hennessey replied. "Get ready, Chloe. It's time to meet baby number two. Don't stop pushing until I tell you to."

"I can't."

"Think of this as a training exercise for the race with Tristan. You can see the finish line. Just one last sprint," Matt said.

"This is *not* a horse race." I clenched my teeth and bore down.

When the second baby appeared, the knots in my shoulders subsided, and I fell back upon the pillows. The nurse wrapped the babies in cotton blankets while Matt watched on.

"I have these," he said to Faith. He produced two pink and blue striped, knit beanies from his back pocket.

The meticulous stitches took me back to my youth. Before I moved to the ranch, I'd sit with Glad on Maggie's front porch in Michigan. I'd read my chapter books to Glad while she knitted hats for the babies at the local hospital.

"Glad wanted them to be a surprise," Matt said.

He checked his phone.

"Your dad, Maggie, and Glad are here." He snapped photos of the babies in Glad's beanies. Then Faith took a few pictures of the four of us together.

We were a family.

CHAPTER 15

"THE BABIES ARE perfect," Faith said. "May 25 will forever be a special day for y'all. Doctor says they're fraternal. And no C-section, no episiotomy, no epidural—you're a trooper. It's like you were made for having babies."

"I'm not sure about that. I do like a challenge though," I said.

Another nurse slipped into the room. Her nametag read Kate. She was heavyset with a gap between her front teeth. Her short dark hair the color of coal was swept to the side, her voice deep and husky.

"Lucky girl," she whispered.

"I am." I had my family, Matt, and a crew waiting for me at home who meant the world to me.

Mom, Dad, Maggie, and Glad waited patiently to meet the new additions. Kate placed baby girl number one on my chest. I'd endured the ride, and the babies prevailed like any McIntyre would.

"I don't want to break her." She squirmed until

her arms were free of the swaddle. When I touched her hand, she held my finger.

"You won't break her, honey. Look into her eyes. She's strong, determined like her momma."

"What else do you know about her?" My insides tingled with fuzzy feelings.

"She won't take no for an answer. Her heart is pure, and she's ready for the world."

"You seem to have more insight than a medium with a crystal ball. You can really see all that?"

"Sure can. Been doing this for thirty-four years. Want to meet baby girl number two?"

"Yes, please."

Kate helped me cradle both babies. "Baby girl number two is mild-mannered. Look at those soulful eyes," she said, her tongue pressed against the back of her teeth. She stroked the baby's forehead. "She's gonna be your quiet one, the thinker, and take after you, cowboy. She has your eyes. Something tells me you could calm the wildest sea."

"That would be me," I said.

Matt was the serene forest filled with hidden gems, and I was the northern Pacific coastline inviting the north wind and unpredictable surf.

Kate patted my hand. "You've done great work here."

My eyes teared up—again. "I never cry. What's wrong with me?"

Mom and Maggie stood in the doorway, waiting for permission to come in.

Mom raised her pointer finger. "Raging hormones and eighteen hours of labor will do that to a girl."

Dad and Glad peeked from behind my mom and Maggie, their gazes bright and twinkly.

"Your dad's been at the nurses' station the whole time. He hasn't changed," Mom said.

"I can still read a chart." Dad's upbeat tone didn't mask his antsy energy. His boot heels tapped against the tiled hospital floor in his usual cowboy style.

"The girls are so tiny," Maggie said with the slightest tremble in her voice.

Baby girl number one's whimper turned to a scowl. Her scrunched expression tugged at my heartstrings. I wanted her to be happy. Matt took her from me and held her close.

"I don't think she's sure about being here," I said.

"We've been waiting for you," he whispered.

"It's like they already know us."

"They certainly do. They're spectacular. So gorgeous." Glad wrapped her arm around Maggie's waist.

"I can't believe you made them beanies," I said.

"I've made so many, the pattern is forever ingrained. Even with these gnarled fingers, I've managed to eke out a few more." Glad raised her hands. She splayed her fingers, her pointers crooked from arthritis and years of doing what Glad did best, caring for others.

Dr. Hennessey entered the room and stood at the foot of my bed. I introduced her to my family.

"We've met." Dad shook her hand.

She peered over the rim of her glasses. "Your dad's very helpful."

"Oh yes, he is." Mom's sarcastic reaction didn't go unnoticed.

"Chloe mentioned you sewed up Matt's head after a fall. Nice work." Dr. Hennessey peered through her glasses like Glad did when she was having trouble focusing.

"Maybe one of these little ones will be a doctor when she grows up. May I?" Dad opened his arms. Tenderness spilled from his gaze.

"The babies' stats look great. Baby girl number one weighs six pounds, two ounces. Number two, six pounds on the dot." Dr. Hennessey leafed through the papers on her clipboard.

"I'm exhausted." I handed baby girl number two to my dad. He whispered sweet welcoming words to her, then kissed her fuzzy head. Glad handed me a tissue, and I dabbed my eyes. Never had I ever dreamed of seeing my father holding a baby, let alone mine.

"We'll be outside if you need us. You did great." Mom kissed my cheek, then left the room with Maggie and Glad.

Matt attempted to comfort baby girl number one, who squirmed and cried. "She sure does have a set of lungs," he said.

"Yes, she does," I replied, hoping she'd stop fussing.

Dr. Hennessey, who was discussing my orders with Faith, glanced over. "They come how they come. Welcome to your next stop in the circle of life. You'll be fine, and so will they. I have no doubts." She and Faith resumed their discussion.

"What's the matter? You look upset." Matt said, caressing my cheek.

"We don't have names." My chin quivered.

"It's okay. Look, the sun is coming up. We could call the girls 311 and 313 until they get proper names," he suggested.

"I love the calves very much, but *no*." Waves of warm sunlight streamed through the blinds. "I wish Grandpa and Ida May were here," I said between sobs.

"You know they are." Matt rocked unhappy baby girl number one. He gladly surrendered her to Faith when she offered to help.

Dad patted Matt on the back. "Congratulations, son." Then he kissed my forehead. "I love you, sweetheart. You did good work. I'll be outside."

"I love you, too, Dad." I plucked two more tissues from the box and blew my nose.

"What would make you want to name them after cattle?" Kate asked.

"We have these two calves who escape from the field to come see me. They're so sweet."

Kate checked my vitals. Dr. Hennessey came back in and sat on the edge of the bed. "You've got quite a family. And now you've added two baby girls to the brood. Looks like Faith has the magic touch with number one. She can't keep her eyes open." Dr. Hennessey stroked the baby's hand.

I scooted myself up in bed and held my daughter while Faith instructed me on how to nurse. "This isn't as strange as I thought it would be," I said.

"Like I said before, you're a natural." Faith straightened the nightstand cluttered with empty cups and tissue.

Matt buried his hands in his pockets; his expression gave off an uncomfortable vibe.

"There's nothing to be embarrassed about," Kate said. "These two little ladies are remarkable. Some babies come out screaming and don't stop until they're eighteen." She patted Matt's arm. "I'm messing with you, sugar. We do get some screamers though. These two are nothing compared to the ones with colic right from the get-go."

"How will we know if the girls are colicky?" I shifted the baby in my arms and repositioned myself in the messy sheets.

"You'll know, sugar. They cry like bleating sheep and don't stop. With my first one, I didn't sleep for two years."

The color drained from Matt's face.

FOR THE NEXT two days, Matt stayed with me nearly twenty-four seven. On the third day, he went home to shower and sleep in his own bed. A drop in baby girl number two's sugar resulted in a delayed discharge. The extra two days in bed left me restless to get home for Maggie and Glad's cooking and my own bed. Mom's reassurance that everything was fine back at the ranch didn't ease my racing mind. When baby girl number two was cleared to go home, I got dressed and eagerly waited for Matt and Dad to come get us.

They loaded us, the stuffed toys, and flowers into the SUV. I sat in the back seat, sandwiched between the girls. I held their tiny hands and imagined a time when they'd be grown up, too independent for their momma's advice.

"The babies don't count as strays, do they, Dad?" We were at nearly forty horses, which made a dent we weren't used to in the budget. I'd find at least ten of them, if not more, rightful owners once the babies were settled.

"Nope." He laughed. "It's awfully quiet back there."

"Let's not jinx it." I straightened their beanies.

The nurses had helped me identify the subtle differences between the girls. Even then, Matt and I agreed to color code their wardrobes until we got the hang of telling them apart. Baby girl number one would wear pink, and number two would wear yellow. During one of Glad's hospital visits, she'd brought her embroidery thread and marked each beanie with the numerals one and two in corresponding colors.

Dad and Matt discussed cattle, horses, and the list of chores as we neared the ranch.

"We're almost there," I told the girls. Baby girl

number one's eyes grew wide.

"You know, they're gonna need names. We can't keep calling them one and two," Dad said, glancing in the rearview mirror.

"We'll figure it out," I said.

I rolled down my window and listened to the river, the same river that took down Matt, the river that brought life to our ranch, the river that masked hidden dangers beneath the rocks if you weren't careful. White clouds dotted the endless blue sky, and the thermostat read fifty-eight degrees.

"We're here," I said to baby girl two, who stretched and squinted into the light. "This is where you're gonna live. The horses and cattle are extra special, like you. I'll teach you to rope, ride, and fish. It's spring outside, the land's sparse covering is turning green like it does every year, and when you least expect it, yellows, blues, and wild purple hues will take over the landscape. Thistle is my favorite."

"Those two aren't going to know what hit 'em," Dad said. "You've got everything planned." His smile blossomed in the rearview mirror like summer wildflowers on a hot day. "I'm sure they've got plans of their own." Dad beeped the horn to announce our arrival. "I seem to remember a little girl who had her own agenda when her mother and I brought her home from the hospital. Those two may be petite, but they'll have big ideas. They're coming up with a master plan as we speak. They'll have ideas you never thought of. Ideas that'll keep you on your toes and make you question your purpose. Ideas that you wish you could've predicted and avoided. Ideas that'll scare the hell out of you," Dad rambled as he parked the truck in the drive.

"Thanks, John. We hadn't thought of all that." Matt got out of the truck. The corners of his mouth turned down.

"Another feel-good moment brought to you by John McIntyre." I unbuckled my seat belt. "I'm sure Dad's got more insight tucked up his sleeve."

"Just keeping it real," he said.

Matt opened the back door and helped me get the girls out of the SUV. "Can't wait to sleep in my own bed tonight."

Dad cooed at baby girl one and continued his narrative. "She's the spitting image of you, Chloe."

Grateful to be home, I breathed in the fresh air and took a moment to enjoy the breeze kissing my cheeks.

Glad waved from the front steps of the main house, then rang the triangular cast-iron dinner bell hanging at the end of the porch. "Home cooking served here," she called.

"Hey, bosslady," Tristan said. The fringe on his chaps swished to an easy gait. "Welcome home."

"Great to be here. Being cooped up in that hospital was driving me nuts. But we're here now, and the girls are both healthy." I held Tristan's gaze, trying to figure out how he felt about meeting the babies. Did he think of James every time he saw a young child?

"Woo-wee, you're gonna have your hands full for some time," he said. "Silas is waiting for your call."

I glanced at Matt.

"No, Chloe," he said. "Silas has other work. We'll find a nanny."

We went inside. Maggie and Mom had the table set for lunch. In the center, on Maggie's favorite crystal serving platter, was a cake with the girls' pictures on it. Pink balloons and streamers filled the dining room.

Everyone hovered around. "Surprise!"

Mom cooed at the babies while Maggie and Glad added the final touches to the lunch spread. Mom's sideways glance caught my attention.

"Any bites on the nanny position?" I asked.

"Unfortunately, no," Mom said.

"Maria never called back?"

"Sorry, sweetheart."

"Don't worry, we'll find someone," Matt said.

"If you don't, I'm free. Hermione and I are still ahead of schedule."

Trout came in with a boisterous hello. The dogs followed him. "Look who finally made it to the party." Trout gravitated toward the girls. "Boy, would your granddaddy and Ida May be sweet on these two. Good work, kid."

When his gaze met Mom's, his smile flatlined. I watched the cool exchange and sat down at the table. There was more than a misunderstanding between them. I'd never seen Trout back down from conflict.

I made myself a turkey sandwich and loaded my plate with fruit.

"We've got huckleberry pie and cake for dessert. We sure do know how to eat," Glad said. "It's a wonder I'm not as big as a house."

"Looks like those babies aren't the only hungry ones." Tristan pulled out a chair, sat, and covered his lap with the linen napkin. "Gracious, girl."

I'd taken one bite, and the crying commenced. "Well, this was a short lunch. I'll be in the den." I excused myself, took baby girl number one from her carrier, sat in one of Dad's comfy leather chairs, and nursed her. I closed my eyes, thinking about the turkey sandwich I'd made.

Matt shut the door and sat on the armrest. "You okay?"

"As long as she's quiet, I'm good." I stroked my daughter's silky, pure skin. "Speaking of quiet, did you notice how quickly Trout lost his spunk around my mother? Did something else happen while I was gone?"

"I don't think so. Trout hasn't mentioned anything, and Maggie, Glad, and your dad had a good talk with her about that day at the river. She even apologized to Quinn and Tristan. Chloe—"

"I know," I answered.

"I didn't say anything."

"You didn't have to. Trout and Mom will work it out sooner or later without me."

As soon as baby girl one fell asleep, baby girl number two's cries echoed through the house.

CHAPTER 16

THE BABIES AND I had made it through our first ten days home. I'd been at the babies' beck and call and missed my morning wrangling routine. Thank goodness my mother's intention for an extended visit hadn't waned. She waited on me and rocked the babies in between talking to Hermione and working on her sketches. With things on an even keel, I thought it best to shake loose from the interruption and reclaim my schedule.

I tiptoed downstairs before sunrise, the wooden floor cool against the soles of my feet. I ran my hand over the mantel, finding my way. I picked up my camera from the ottoman, careful not to make a sound.

I slipped into my studded boots in the mud-room, then put on my shearling jacket over my nightgown and unlocked the back door. The click of the deadbolt echoed in the night air. Outside was a world with no walls, a world ruled by nature and animals, a place I did my best thinking.

The chilly air cooled my cheeks. I was out of the house. An escapee, like 311 and 313. Hair swirled around my face. I gathered it in a ponytail and braided it, securing it with the hair tie around my wrist. The glow of the moon lit the path to the pen where I'd find the calves sleeping. My boots scuffed along the ground.

I crouched near the split rail fence to photograph them. I wasn't sure if the pictures would even come out, but Montana in the wee hours of the morning was as exquisite as any other time of day.

"Lucky dogies," I whispered to myself, leaning on the fence before 311 whipped her head around and peered at me. I held my hand out to her. "It's me. Chloe."

Her eyes grew wide, and she stood on sleepy legs. I climbed between the rails. The tall grass tickled my shins. "Hi, baby girl." I stroked her shoulder. "I'm sorry I haven't been here. Hope the boys are treating you okay."

"We are," Tristan said, stepping from the shadows. "What are you doing out here?"

"My mother is with the babies, and I needed a moment to myself." I peered through the viewfinder and snapped his photo.

"My mom knows how to sing a lullaby. I

don't. Learning how to change diapers is like learning a foreign language. Calming the cries is a full-time job. When they stop, there's a moment of relief, then I anxiously await the next bout. Oh, and do you know what else?" I climbed out of the pen. "Those girls are going to get attached to my mom. When she leaves, what will I do?"

"You mean, *you'll* get attached."

"Exactly," I whispered.

"You'll go on running this place with your dad. You'll take care of the girls and plan your next get-together." He paused and took the camera from around my neck. "You're sleep-deprived. Stop worrying and make the best of right now." A dark shadow washed over Tristan's gaze.

Calf 313 stood and nudged me.

"When Vivian and I brought James home from the hospital, he cried nonstop. It took him at least six months to settle down and get the hang of living on the outside." Tristan rubbed his chin, then glanced up to the lingering stars getting their last licks in before the morning light.

I held up two fingers. "There are two babies," I said. The words popped.

"I know. I've met them. And, by the grace of God, you got to bring them home."

"That's it," I said.

"What's it?" Tristan leaned against the fence. The collar of his leather coat framed his face. The reflection of the moon lit his genuine nature, and I felt Vivian and James at my back, filling the man they loved with light.

"By the grace of Ida May, we have two little girls. Number one should be Gracie May, and, yes, I'm tired. This learning curve is steep." I scratched 311's ears. "Why are you up so early, Tristan?"

"Can't sleep. Can't sleep most nights. Wish I could, because then I'd get to see them." He lifted his chin to the heavens.

"See who?" I knew who he meant but wanted to hear him say their names one more time. They deserved to hear their names from the man who loved them back.

"Viv and James. I used to dream about them a lot. Now they come less often." His words trailed off. "Without them, I can't sleep."

"You won't forget them. They'll always be with you like my grandpa and Ida May are with me. Vivian is a pretty name. I bet she was beautiful."

"She was."

I leaned in and kissed him on the cheek.

He closed his eyes before speaking. "Why did you do that?"

I held his chin in the palm of my hand. He slowly opened his eyes, revealing the sentiment he worked so hard to hide.

"Because she asked me to," I said.

He pushed his hat back. "Chloe—" His Adam's apple quivered.

"What?" I took the camera back from him.

"You're something else. Thank you."

"That's what friends are for." I paused. "But this soft moment doesn't mean I'm gonna feel sorry for you when I get back on Gypsy and whop you in that race. We owe her." I snapped a picture of his profile as he stared into the distance. The glint in his eye captured the passion for his lost family and the Montana life that kept them close.

I hoped I would be lucky enough to possess a fraction of his stamina.

Tristan and I strolled to the empty pasture near the barn. Matt waited at the fence line. Steam rose from his coffee like early morning fog. The three of us soaked in the warm, yellow hues of the new dawn. The blanket of haze drifted away with the sunrise. The horses roamed the distant hillside, waiting for their escort home.

Matt kissed my cheek. "Good morning, Momma. Are the girls okay?"

"According to my inner clock, I have a few

more minutes until I'm needed."

"Remember those instincts when you're flustered," Matt said.

I spotted Gypsy between two scraggly pines as tough as the two wranglers by my side. Mist rose from her back as she navigated the slope.

"What do you think about the name Gracie May?"

Matt breathed it in, savoring it like it was the last scent of sage before the snow.

"Sounds mighty fine. Is that number one or two?"

"On the count of three, we'll hold up our fingers to see if we agree on which girl it fits," I said.

"That's an unusual way to decide names." Tristan blew away the chill from his hands. "You two let me know how this turns out. I've got horses to saddle."

"I'll be along in a few." Matt sipped his coffee then set his cup on the fence post. "Okay, I've thought about it. On the count of three."

We each fisted a hand, counted to three and held up one finger. A thread of joy pulled at the seam of my lips.

"It's settled. Number one is Gracie May. Have you thought about last names, Momma?"

"What do you think about McIntyre-Cooper?"

"We don't have to make a decision now, but I like it."

"I'm gonna check on the girls and get the day started." I drew my jacket tight, tucking my chin into the fleece collar. Matt played with the tassel of my braid.

"I can't wait to see you back up on a horse."

"That'll be a great day," I said. "And thanks."

"For what?"

"For letting me be me." I leaned in and kissed him on the cheek. "You smell good."

"I wish I could say the same about you. You kind of smell like spit-up."

"On that note, I'm gonna go, but not before I tell you, I can't resist a cowboy on a horse." I clicked my tongue at him. "By the way, that cowboy is you." I turned on a heel. My nightgown swished against my shins like the shabby chic dress I imagined my mother designing with me in mind.

I kicked off my boots at the back door and went upstairs. Mom's room was dark. When I checked in on the girls, Gracie May was wide awake. Her gaze seemed to ask me where I'd been. I picked her up, crept into my room, and snuggled with her in bed.

"Why do you cry so much?" I caressed her tiny fingers. "Papa and I decided to name you Gracie

May because, by the grace of God, you defied all precautions and found your way home. May was your great-grandma's middle name. She ran the ranch with your great-grandpa, Winston." I kissed her hand.

"Let's bundle you up, and we'll watch the horses. Waking before sunrise means learning early what ranching is all about." Lola joined us on the bed to cuddle. She had turned into some cattle dog. If she could split her time between the field and home, so could I.

The rising sun lit the horizon. If we didn't get moving, we'd miss the morning run, and I wanted to see my Gypsy lead the herd. After burping Gracie, I laid her in the center of the bed. Lola circled Gracie twice, then laid next to her.

I slipped out of my nightgown and into a pair of jeans, a button-down plaid flannel shirt, and a fleece. I swaddled my daughter in a cottony blanket before tiptoeing into the hallway with her cradled close to my body.

Mom's bedroom door was open, and I peeked inside. She'd drawn the drapes to let in the light and opened a suitcase filled with fabric samples and art supplies. Looking up from my father's childhood desk, she pushed her glasses to her forehead.

"I had no clue you had all this stuff with you,"

I said. She'd laid groups of pencils and markers beneath the fabric to match the colors. Inquisitive, I stepped into the room. I'd never witnessed such an organized disarray around her.

"Hermione and I have a meeting later today. Thank goodness for technology." She sipped coffee from a mug. "I like your drawings at the back of my sketchbook. You've got hidden talent."

"Hope I didn't goof up your work. I thought I'd take Gracie May outside with me to watch the horses. Number two is still sleeping."

"My work is fine, and it sounds like someone has a very country name." Mom caressed Gracie May's cheek.

"Good, because that's what we are. Grandma McIntyre's middle name was May."

"I remember. Your dad was crushed when she passed away. He loved her very much."

"I thought she passed before you two knew each other."

"She did; your dad was in high school. He talked about her a lot when you were born. Your granddad wasn't the only one with a head for raising cattle. Without Ida May's influence, the 617 Ranch might not have made it. She and Winston were quite the couple."

"They were indeed." A familiar shiver ran

down my spine. "I'll take the radio."

"Leave my door open. I'll keep an eye on number two."

I padded downstairs and buckled Gracie May into her carrier. "Here we go. I can feel the horses in my bones. Don't be scared. Their hooves sound like thunder, but we won't get too close." Tiny gurgling noises escaped her perfect pink lips. I slipped my feet back into my boots and hung the camera across my body.

When Gracie and I went outside, Samson was on the deck. Lola scooted past me, circled Samson until he poked Lola with his stubby snout and yipped. Samson appeared pleased with his intervention and waddled beside me as we walked down the drive toward the barn. Lola ran under the fence rail when she saw Quinn ride out. Samson stayed with me, happy to keep his distance from the thundering hooves.

I set the carrier on the ground, scooped Gracie May up, and held her close to my chest. "You're going to love the horses. Without a doubt." Her thin lip curled. "That's my girl."

Maggie joined us. Her tired gaze revived with the sight of my sweet girl. "Late night?"

"I worked on my book until three in the morning. These creative urges hit me at the strangest times." Maggie reached for the camera. "Do you mind?"

"Not at all." I watched Matt, Silas, and Tristan comb the hillside for stragglers. Dad manned the gate. The click of the aperture was like a ticking clock, our chronicles starting now. I peered at Maggie. She positioned my messy braid over my collarbone. "Baby girl number one has a name," I said.

Maggie lowered the camera. "Do tell."

"Meet Gracie May."

"Hello, Gracie May." Maggie kissed Gracie's button nose. "May goodness and generosity rule your world, little one. You've got a big life ahead of you."

"We certainly do."

I thought about Mom, her room scattered with work. The drawings. Her visions created with color, imagination, backstory I never understood. Until now.

I nuzzled Gracie close and imagined a time when the nurse laid me on my mother's chest. Our hearts beating together, a united tempo like an easy canter when the sun rose and a hard day's work awaited. Gracie's tiny breaths filled the space between us.

Maggie adjusted the camera setting and

snapped more pictures. Gracie fidgeted, working herself free from the blanket I'd wrapped her in.

"I think we've established you want your arms outside of the blanket." I kissed Gracie's nose. "I would, too. Let's make this work."

With Maggie's help, I wrapped Gracie back up, supported her head, and gazed into her green-blue eyes.

"Soon you'll be able to see what I see. For now, listen to my voice and see through me. The mountains are pointy and poke the sky above our heads. The grass is green and tickles your skin. The blanket of fog drifts around us like a suspended band of feathers. The sun is bright and pushes the night away when it's time to get up."

"She really is the spitting image of you," Maggie said. "She's gorgeous. I wonder if Bradley will ever have children." Maggie focused the camera on the sunrise.

"Do you want him to?"

"Having children is his decision. I wouldn't want him to have children because I want grand-children."

"Clearly, someone else decided for Matt and me. If Bradley doesn't, I've got you covered, Grandma." Gracie settled down and yawned.

Maggie's eyes brimmed with tears.

"Are you crying because I called you Grandma or because my mother claimed the title of Coco first?"

Maggie laughed. "Grandma or whatever other nickname the girls come up with will be an honor."

In the distance, Dad opened the gate and the horses bounded through the field. "Here they come." My heart raced as Gypsy bolted to the front of the herd.

"Gypsy craves your attention like children want their mothers."

"I see her every day, but there's something to be said about alone time." I couldn't blame her for her persnickety attitude. Talking to my best girl in the corral wasn't the same as riding in the fields together, discussing the day's work and personal woes.

Tristan on Hitch sprinted alongside the charging horses. Manes slashed the hovering fog. Maggie covered Gracie's ears. Matt on Trigger and Dad on Breeze, two men with serious mugs ready for another day of wrangling and ranching, cantered in stride. They slowed about fifty yards away, then trotted over to us.

"Whoa." Dad pulled back on Breeze's's reins. Steam billowed from her nostrils in the chilly air.

She whinnied, her head bobbing to the easy stride, her ears back when she saw Maggie. "What are you three doing out here?"

"Baby girl number one was up, so we came out," I said. "Dad, I'd like you to meet Gracie May."

"Glad to meet you, Gracie May." Dad nudged his hat back from his forehead. Hidden dimples emerged, his tone mighty pleased. Maggie took Gracie's hand and helped her wave at him.

Dad dismounted and looped the reins around the fence rail. He held Maggie's stare. "Hi there," he said. Maggie focused the camera on him and took his picture. He climbed through the fence and kissed her.

"Hi, cowboy." Her cheeks were aglow with more than the sunrise.

I rocked Gracie May gently and whispered the words of the lullaby I'd heard Mom singing.

"We'll see you two later," I said. Gracie and I would take our time getting back home. Mom had said she'd forgotten what it was like to watch a sleeping baby in the early morning light. I wanted to make sure I didn't.

Had I ever *really* slept as a child? I felt as if I'd been awake my whole life, never wanting to miss a moment.

"I'll bring the baby carrier and the camera back

to the house in a bit," Maggie said.

Birds chirped their morning tunes, and the dew slid into the earth from the backs of green blades of grass. Mom peered out the upstairs window. She rocked baby girl number two in her arms. I no longer wished my mom to have a different life, a life that suited my needs. This visit had become a milestone in our relationship.

A crescendo of muffled wails penetrated the panes of glass between us. By the time I got inside, Mom had made her way to the living room. She sang and rocked inconsolable baby girl number two, her focus clearly on her granddaughter and not the projects strewn across the floor of her bedroom. I placed Gracie in her Moses basket, tucked her in, and kicked off my boots.

"I don't know how they sleep through each other's cries." I relieved my mother and made myself comfortable on the sofa.

"Mom, was I a good baby?"

"Yes, Chloe. You were giggly, funny, independent, stubborn, loving. All the things you are now."

"Did I ever sleep?"

"Eventually, and so will they." She twisted her hair around her finger.

"Who taught you how to sing lullabies and

soothe fussing babies? I don't think I have those genes."

"Your father, and yes, you do." The corner of her mouth lifted, and she played with the tie of her bathrobe. "Winston told your dad stories about Ida May when he couldn't remember the gaps in time. I'm sure I didn't measure up to your dad's memories of his mother."

"I'm sorry you think that." I craved backstory. "Tell me more about your mom." I stroked number two's cheek as she nursed.

"She wanted me to go to college. I took classes but didn't get a degree. She smoked cigarettes, wore lipstick the color of tangerines, and kitten heels. She worked as a secretary, had an affair with her boss after my father died, but she didn't know I knew. She loved him. He left her for someone younger and broke her heart. She packed me bologna sandwiches with ketchup for lunch and watched cartoons with me on Saturday morning before we went grocery shopping together. She took me shopping for a new Easter dress every year. We wore white patent leather Mary Janes and matching hats to church. When I went to junior high, we still shopped for Sunday dresses, but I'd given up my Mary Janes for pumps, and I talked my mother out of wearing matching hats."

"I like those stories about her better than the ones you told me before."

"Me too."

Mom disappeared into the kitchen, then returned with a cup of tea. She sat at the opposite end of the sofa, kicked off her slippers, and propped her feet up on the ottoman.

"I'm going to shower after I drink this. Then it'll be your turn. When the girls nap today, you should, too."

"Okay." I gladly accepted my mom's advice.

The sound of the shower wafted through the house like a gentle spring rain. Number two stared up at me. "Your sister has my grandma's middle name. Your middle name should be Jean, like Coco's. How do you feel about Lillian Jean?"

She closed her eyes and brought her tiny hands to her chest. I took her angelic expression as a *yes*.

CHAPTER 17

L ILLIAN SLEPT IN the crook of my arm. Mom came downstairs after her shower and sat beside me on the sofa. She tucked her feet beneath her, her knees visible through her distressed jeans, her plain yellow tee the color of summer buttercups, her hair tied in a messy bun.

I scooched to the edge of the sofa and placed Lillian in the bassinet. The knot between my shoulders pinched. Mom picked up the copy of *La Chic* and leafed to the page where she and Hermione posed together in the favorite pieces of their collection. She pointed to the white linen tunic.

"The embroidery along this scalloped neckline is divine. You'd think the white stitches would get lost against the white fabric. But we used a flexible slubby thread. Gives texture and volume to the stitching. Flawless design."

I leaned closer to get a better look. "I can't believe I inspired this."

"You did. Why would you doubt that?" She held up her hand and lowered her lashes. "Don't answer that."

"Where can I get one?"

"I'll take care of it." Mom smiled. "Why don't you shower before the girls wake up?"

"Remember when I suggested you design bandannas? I tucked images of thistle, lupine, Indian paintbrushes—flowers you'd find around here—in the back of your sketchbook."

"I found them with your sketches. My daughter the wrangler is letting her fashion chops shine. I shared your ideas with Hermione. She approves. She loves the flowers and plants you chose. We're thinking beyond the bandanna. Neckerchiefs, silk scarves."

"I like."

"We could work on the designs together. Think about it. I won't push you." She straightened her shoulders. "I found the teardrops you drew, too."

"Let's not go backward, Mom. Isn't that what we agreed we wouldn't do while you were here? You've apologized already." I massaged my neck. "I won't be long in the shower unless I fall asleep. Oh, I've got an idea for number two's name. I'll run it by Matt and get back to you."

Mom whispered to baby girl two, "Did you hear that? You're gonna get a name. Looks like your momma has her mind made up, and she usually gets what she wants. So do I."

I like the way *momma* rolled from my mother's tongue.

"Should I be worried?"

"Not this time, daughter."

Baby girl number two yawned and closed her eyes, her pink cheeks like rosy dollops of sweetness.

"Chloe, *someone* knew your father and I needed you too."

I didn't change the subject. I'd take those words with me on every ride, down every dirt road, and tuck them beneath my pillow when I slept.

"GRACIE MAY AND Lillian Jean," I said to myself in the bathroom mirror before sliding the bandanna from my head. The Montana morning dew did wonders for my skin, another million-dollar idea for Mom to bottle and market to the world.

I stepped into the steamy shower. The pulsating water massaged my shoulders while I replayed the conversation I'd just had with my mom. The kindness and genuine sentiment validated my decision to start anew with her. Dad was right when he said she'd surprise me.

I toweled off, went to my bedroom, and got

dressed. Matt knocked before poking his head into the room.

"Your momma sent me up here. She said you've named baby girl number two and wants to know if it's a go or not." He shut the door behind him and sat in the leather chair next to the fireplace.

"I was thinking Lillian Jean. Jean is from my mom's side of the family, and Lillian because she looks like a Lillian to me. Does she look like a Lillian to you? Too old-fashioned? We could call her Lil or Lilly."

"It's more than okay. We could use a little old-fashioned. Sometimes things move too quickly," he said.

"Really?" I wrinkled up my nose at him. "You don't mind that the names didn't come from your family? I know you loved your adoptive mom very much."

"She'll always be Mom to me. The girls will have McIntyre-Cooper. We're not hitched, and they should know who their daddy is."

"They'll definitely know their daddy." I put on my necklace and fingered the silver heart charm, then inspected Matt's stitches. "Your head looks good. Try not to get hurt anymore. And Matt—"

"What?"

"I hope everything between us is as easy as naming the girls." I made the bed and fluffed the pillows.

"It probably won't be, but with your perseverance and my brawn, we can get through anything. Choose your hard, Chloe McIntyre."

I unwrapped the towel from my wet hair and tossed it at him. He stood and draped it over his shoulders like a cape, then planted his hands on his hips.

"Nice. The girls will be very excited to know their papa is a superhero."

"You mean Gracie May and Lillian Jean," he said with a smile. "Gracie and Lil. Lil and Gracie. Nice, very nice."

"Yes. I mean Gracie and Lil," I said.

"Well, you can share that with your mother. I've got work to do, and they say a storm is rolling in. We can only do the best we can do. I've got your back, cowgirl."

Matt snapped my backside with the towel, then opened the door. Mom stood in the hallway with baby girl two.

"Well. Does she have a name?"

"Lillian Jean. Thought maybe she should have something from your family, too." Mom's pinched stare was unnerving. "What? Don't you like it?"

Mom hemmed and hawed.

"Seriously, what's wrong?" I asked.

"So, baby girl number two will be Lillian Jean."

"Yes, McIntyre-Cooper."

"Lillian Jean McIntyre-Cooper," she said and repeated it three times. Lil scrunched up her face. Her pouty, breathy sobs were my clue she wanted to be fed. I took her from my mom, went into the babies' room, and made myself comfortable in the rocking chair. Matt gave Lil a quick kiss and ducked out. Mom stood over me fiddling with Lil's yellow booties.

"What do you *really* think, Mom?"

"Sounds like Montana has gained another force to be reckoned with." She leaned against the doorjamb and crossed her arms. "I'll let you two have some privacy."

"Come on, Lillian Jean, don't be so fussy." Staring at her profile, I couldn't help but think maybe she had some of my mom's genes after all.

MOM STAYED IN her bedroom working on designs and business logistics like she did most afternoons. I left a lunch tray outside her door around two o'clock each day. Nutrition took a back seat to her work, but I made sure she ate. She had settled into a routine. She appeared to be happier. She drank less wine in the evenings, and I didn't worry as much. Our newfound equilibrium made for a happy home.

Gracie and Lil slept in the bassinets in the living room. I put my feet up with the intent to finish Trout's chapter book. The back door closed with a thud, and Glad padded in. I peeked beneath my lashes as she hovered over me like an angel. Her age showed in the sunlight coming through the shutters. I traced the lines in her skin on the back of her hand.

"Do you think wrinkles represent memories?" I met her stare. "You'd think my mom would have some deep ones. What if she's erasing them with procedures and beauty creams?"

"I believe wrinkles hold memories. I surmise she hides her wrinkles somewhere else, child. We all have our secrets," Glad said.

"I worry about her."

"You always have."

"My mom started seeing a therapist after my last visit."

"Good for her. That's a big step." Glad fidgeted with her wedding band. "Am I supposed to know all this?"

"I'm not sure what she's told Dad or Maggie."

"I won't say anything." Glad paused. "Your mom is one complex woman. You've handled yourself well. It's good she's here."

I held Glad's hand. "We named the babies this morning. Baby girl number one is Gracie May and baby girl number two is Lillian Jean."

"Thank goodness. The numbers were getting old. I'll remove them from their beanies and embroider their initials."

There was a knock at the back door. Then the lackadaisical shuffle of footsteps drifted through the kitchen. My nerves prickled, and I put my finger to my lips.

"Is anyone home?" the stranger with the deep voice said.

I jumped up, grabbed the poker from the hearth, and held it over my head, ready to swing. Glad's stare widened. I waited for the intruder to make his way into the living room. My pulse raced.

Suddenly, Mom yelled, "No!" as she rushed in.

The man snatched the poker from me, and I let out a shriek, pulled my arm back, and balled my fingers into a fist. Before Mom could stop me, I punched him.

"Chloe! He's here to see me."

The man dropped the poker, held the bridge of his nose, and groaned. Excruciating pain shot up my arm—nothing like childbirth though, and I was okay with that. I shook out my hand. Glad rushed over to Gracie and Lil, who stirred with the chaos.

"Who lets themselves into a stranger's house?" Not ready to back down, I grabbed the poker again.

Mom hurried over to check his face. "I told him to. I didn't want him to wake the babies."

"Now, now, girlies." Glad stepped between the bassinets, shushing Gracie and Lil. "It's all right. Your momma carries a mean wallop, so I'd mind my manners if I were you."

I stepped back and scowled at our visitor.

Glad handed him the tissue box from the otto-man, stepped closer to me, and touched my forehead. "Now those are wrinkles, kiddo. Bet you'll remember this for a long time. I suppose *they* will too."

"You didn't tell me we were having company." I glanced at Mom, then to her *friend*, noting his designer loafers, madras plaid shirt, white pants, chiseled jaw, and tanner-than-tan complexion. I could only deduce he was from Cali.

"I'm staying down the road." He blotted his nose with tissue.

"What are you thinking, Chloe?" Mom's blue gaze clouded over.

"How was I supposed to know he's your friend?"

"You could've asked who was there," Mom scolded.

"Like I'm going to lead with pleasantries when there's a stranger in my house."

"That's not what I meant." Mom's voice trailed off as she put her arm around the tall, sandy-haired man.

"You should announce yourself," I said.

"Chloe!" Mom snapped and helped her friend to the sofa.

"If I'm ever in need of a bouncer, I'll give you a call," he said.

The girls fussed. Glad picked up Gracie and rocked her. I cuddled Lil and held her close until the tears subsided.

"Chloe, this is Jeffrey Sands." Mom returned the poker to the wrought iron stand.

"Hi, Jeffrey Sands. I'm the incorrigible daughter who just had twins, Chloe McIntyre. I'm a bit overprotective."

Jeffrey dabbed his nose. "You're right, I should've announced myself or called your mother from outside. You've got a mean right hook."

"Flattery won't win me over. It's been my experience that when people lead with a sneaky entrance and a compliment, they're fishing for something." I looked at my mom. "Is this the pilot you met on the flight here?"

She bit her thumbnail and shook her head. My internal trust meter told me to proceed with caution and back away until I got the whole story about this guy. But as much as I wanted to hash it out with Mom right then, the girls needed attention, and I wouldn't ignore them.

"If you'll excuse me, family comes first." I stepped closer to my mother. "I expect you'll fill me in when I'm not preoccupied. We've worked so hard to get here."

Mom and Mr. Sands went outside. They stood beneath the shade tree in the yard, talking. I covered the ottoman with one of the blankets my mom had given the girls and changed Lil's diaper, keeping my mom and Sands in view.

"Who is that guy? And what is he up to?" I played with Lil's toes, pretending each one was a piggy.

"I think Gracie's got the answer to your question, but it's in her pants and doesn't smell good," Glad said.

"I think Lil agrees, and so do I."

CHAPTER 18

I STOOD AT the living room window, watching the clouds drift in the distance. Their shadows rolled over the mountains. Patches of sunlight appeared to be shooing them away. My mom and her friend had majestic scenery for whatever it was they chatted about beneath the shade tree.

"We both know this isn't some nonchalant visit. Mr. Sands is not her boyfriend. He's not her therapist."

Glad peered at me, over the rim of the pink readers balanced on the tip of her nose, like she used to when I was a kid and trouble brewed.

"Don't look at me like that. You know I'm right."

"Everything happens for a reason." She tugged at the hem of her shirt.

"I'm such a sucker."

"Not really. Just a girl who wants a relationship with her mother."

"She's got a knack for handling the girls. She sings to them and doesn't mind when they cry. She shared things about herself I didn't know. She encouraged me to doodle in her sketchbook, and she asked me to work on new designs with her. She even said she wouldn't push me. She apologized to everyone—maybe not Trout, but I wouldn't know because he's off doing who knows what and I'm staying out of their business, which I should get a gold star for."

"That's quite the list of things in her favor."

Glad cradled my face in her hands and kissed my forehead.

"What's that for?"

"I don't have a gold star."

"Thanks. Looks like Mom and Mr. Sands are headed toward the barn. Do you feel like doing a little babysitting?"

"You really should be resting, Chloe."

"I know." I gave Glad a two-way radio and reminded her how it worked if the girls woke up, then hooked the other radio on my belt. "Call if you need me."

"Ten-four." Her voice echoed in the kitchen.

"You're the best." I blew her a kiss.

"I know," she said. "I expect you back shortly. You need your rest."

"Maybe so, but if Maggie wandered off with a questionable suitor, wouldn't you follow her?"

"You know me too well. I have to say, I've never regretted getting caught."

The sultry afternoon breeze and sun on my shoulders remedied my knotted emotions. Calves 311 and 313 grazed in their pen.

"Hi, girl." I scratched 313's head. She swished her tail and poked me with her nose until I produced one lone piece of sugar from my pocket. "This is all I have." She plucked it from the palm of my hand. "You're so greedy." Then 311 meandered over, a blade of grass hanging from her mouth. I reached for it, and she gobbled it down.

I walked to the barn and peered inside. My boot heels knocked against the timber floor as I inspected the empty stalls.

In the tack room, I ran my hand over the saddle Grandpa had given me for my sixteenth birthday. Birthdays were special around here. It wasn't about being another year older—it was about being another year loved.

My working saddle hung on a lonely peg near the top of the collection. The worn leather was cool to the touch. I rearranged the short stack of saddle blankets, then crouched to pet my favorite barn cat, Coal. Mom was nowhere in sight, let alone that Mr. Sands character.

I stepped from the tack room, exited into the

corral area, and circled around to the original barn Grandpa had built the same year he'd built *my* house. Rows of horseshoes hanging on wooden dowels lined the walls. They'd seen miles of wear and protected the hooves of many fine creatures. I kicked the bale of hay sitting near the stairway. Coal ran across my feet and disappeared upstairs. I followed.

Pockets of light lit the dim space where secrets from the past danced in the specks of dust blanketing the loft. I took the radio from my belt, set it on the trunk, and sat down. The wooden floor made from dense planks was hard against my behind. The far set of windows resembled a jack-o'-lantern's face as daylight shone through the rectangular panes. I imagined my grandparents dancing to soft music at one of the parties they were known to host here.

This was a moment I wanted to share with my mother. If she were here, I would tell her about my daydream to make the loft usable again. She'd see something I didn't. We would agree the faux bear rug could work up here.

I pushed myself up from the floor and grabbed the broom leaning against the wall. Rekindling the magic would be a pricy renovation. I imagined the glow of paper lanterns, twinkle lights, and seeing the starry sky through the wavy panes of glass. My mind reeled with ideas for this place while I swept. Midway through the country tune I hummed, Mom's voice drifted up the stairs.

I heard the words *camera, lighting,* and *crew.* What was Sands doing here? Was Mom planning a shoot? Had she spoken to Dad? How did the 617 Ranch relate to consulting or any of her other projects? Nothing made sense.

I made my presence known. Mom's sideways glance at her friend, Mr. Sandy-pants, ruffled my curiosity further.

"I thought I heard voices," I said.

Mr. Sands touched the bridge of his nose, and I curbed the impulse to smile. My radar still didn't read social visit. "So, what are you two up to?"

Mr. Sands eyed my mother.

"This is a great barn, isn't it? Original. Lots of history. My grandpa built it," I said.

Mom played with loose strands of hair that fell from the bun at her nape. Her glance strayed to Mr. Sands, then back to me.

"Are you two gonna ride? Matt or Quinn could take you out. Quinn's doing errands, but he should be back soon. The weather's holding out—how about a tour of the working barn? We all have degrees, you know. I thought maybe I'd be a vet someday," I rambled.

"Okay, Chloe." Mom's tone dipped in sync with her eyebrows.

"Just trying to make conversation." The radio on the back of my belt crackled with Dad's voice. I answered it and went outside.

"What is it?" Mom scurried behind me. "More loose cattle, a stampede? Is anyone hurt?"

"I don't know. Dad needs the emergency kit." Mom and Sands followed me as I hurried to the drive. I yanked open the door of my granddaddy's vintage truck. Turning the key left in the ignition, I spied Maggie running in my direction. Mom and Mr. Sands scooted into the front seat.

"Where do you two think you're going?"

"With you," Mom said. "You're not supposed to be driving." She tapped her watch.

"What are you doing? I thought you put that thing away." Skeptical that she put it back on to track her steps, I raised a brow.

She glanced at Mr. Sands. "How do you feel about riding in the back?" She tugged at his shirt and pointed to the truck bed.

He and I got out. I called to Maggie, "You have to drive. This is Mr. Sands, a friend of Mom's." I released the tailgate. "It's your only option, Mr. Sands." I smiled as he debated about getting his white pants dirty. His gaze met my mom's through the rear window. He muttered something under his breath and hopped in. I got into the passenger's seat, buckled up, and radioed Glad. "Are the girls okay?"

The radio crackled. "Still sleeping, momma bear," she answered.

"Good. There's an emergency in the field."

Maggie rushed past my door, Dad's doctor bag in hand, and gave the dented exterior a lively slap. Maggie buckled up, put the truck in drive, and we headed out.

"Another exciting ride," my mom said.

"Whatever's going on, when we get there, stay out of the way." I planted my hand on the dashboard.

"Do you have your camera?" She reached beneath the seat, then checked the glovebox. The look in her eyes meant business. Her carefree attitude had slipped away.

"Please stop, Mom. Didn't we just go through this? I don't want anyone getting hurt, including your friend in the back."

Maggie hit a rut, and we all let out a gasp. I looked back to make sure Mr. Sands was still with us.

"What in tarnation is going on?" Maggie

slowed when we got to the north pasture. "I've never seen anything like this. Oh my."

The cattle scattered. They appeared confused, scared. Maggie accelerated. I had an inkling about the problem when I saw Tristan and his wildcard equine, Casanova.

"I'll man the gate." I got out of the truck. Mom followed. I waved Maggie on, slapped the bumper when she'd cleared the gate, and opened the passenger door. "Mom, this isn't a game. Get in. Buckle up. And stay there." Before she could speak, I shushed her. "Stay in this truck until I tell you otherwise." My gaze met Maggie's. "I'm gonna ride in the back with Mr. Sands."

"Got it, bosslady," Maggie said.

After locking the gate, I stood at the rear of the truck, staring at Mr. Sands.

"The sooner you give me a hand up, the sooner we can get going." After getting situated, I tapped the roof of the cab, signaling Maggie I was ready to go.

The last thing we needed was loose cattle. Chasing after 311 and 313 was one thing, but rounding up the rest of them was something else. When they got spooked, convincing them to settle down made for a long day.

Maggie parked the truck behind the trunk of a

cottonwood that had fallen after being struck by lightning last summer. With the medical bag in hand, she pushed open her door.

"What's the matter?" Excitement laced Sands's question. "This is crazy great."

"Plenty is the matter. And this isn't great." My stern tone was far from friendly.

"You'd look good on camera," he said. "Audiences like a strong female with a feminine side."

"You're going to stay in this truck. If you don't, those wranglers you see rounding up those unruly cattle will be roping you, too. They won't be pleased if you take them from their work."

Maggie helped me from the truck bed.

"Why is he telling you that you'd look good on camera?" she asked.

"I don't know, but I intend to find out." I leaned into the open window and stared at my mom. "Why is Mr. Sands here?" Anger tampered the rising quiver. "I meant what I said back at the house, Mom. Family comes first. This is not that. You baited me, and I don't like being baited any more than I like coming in second. And I'm not talking about racing and rodeo. We agreed not to go backward."

Maggie moved to the other side of the fallen tree.

Mom gripped the door handle.

"If anything you've said or done since you got here is genuine"—I covered her hand with mine—"you *will not* open this door."

Maggie yelled for me to join her.

"She's not calling you." I looked up at Sands, who peered down at me with a frown. "Tristan's horse has thrown the herd into a tizzy." I pointed across the field. "Wish I could ride." I held the radio in my hand in case Glad called.

"Why can't you ride?" Sands questioned.

I looked at Mom. "Is this guy serious?"

Dad rode over to Maggie to get the medical bag.

"Scenes like this wouldn't have to be scripted. You're right, Brook. This would make for great television. Is someone hurt? I'd like to see your dad sew someone up."

I looked at Sands. "Don't make me come up there!" I reached into the truck and grabbed my rope from the dashboard.

Maggie yelled as she ran toward me, "Is everything okay, Chloe?"

"No." I said, keeping an eye on Sands. "Is anyone hurt? Where's Matt?"

"Matt's fine. No one's hurt—yet. Tristan's got his hands full. Just want to be prepared."

"Whoa. Casanova is going crazy." I shaded my brow to see him better.

Casanova stood on his hind legs and slashed the air with his front hooves. He squealed and whipped his head around. Tristan's face was hard and focused as he attempted to control his horse. I shaded my eyes from the sun, and the world around me blurred into the landscape when Casanova bucked Tristan from the saddle.

"No!" I balled my fists. "Get out of the truck. Both of you. Now," I ordered. "You want drama, let's get you a front row seat." I opened the truck door and took my mother by the hand.

"Your daughter's a dynamo with great bone structure." Sands scurried down from the truck bed.

Mom covered her face, then peeked through her fingers.

Sands watched with an open jaw and wide eyes. I swore his green irises morphed into dollar signs.

"That wrangler with his face in the dirt has a name." I grabbed Mr. Sands's arm as he reached into his pocket. "This isn't a photo opportunity." I snatched his phone and tucked it in the back pocket of my jeans. "Reach for it and you'll be sorry."

Dad on Breeze circled us. His intense gaze was not to be challenged. He was in control and letting the men do their jobs, and that included me. Today, I was one of them, just like old times.

"Do you need my help, Chloe?" he asked.

"No, Dad. I've got this. I'll call Putnam." I took my phone from my jacket pocket. "You know it's a good day when this thing is connected to the server. Thank goodness the skies cleared." I stepped away from the group, dialed our lawyer, quickly explained the situation, and asked him to call me back. Mom took me by the elbow and brought me closer to the fallen tree.

Casanova stopped rearing up. His nostrils flared with each heavy breath. He lowered his head, then sniffed Tristan.

"Get up," I said. "Come on, get up."

Quinn rode across the field. Tristan called to him to stand down, then Tristan got to his knees.

"I should be out there," I said between gritted teeth.

"What's stopping you?" Sands asked.

Mom grabbed his arm and shook her head. "Please. Not now."

"Not ever." I waggled my pointer finger at him as we stood toe to toe. "There isn't anything about my ranch you can have or use. Including my mother."

I took his phone from my back pocket, dropped it in the dirt, and stepped on it. "Send me the bill." With my heel, I ground it into the earth until the screen cracked.

"I knew these studded boots would come in handy."

"Chloe—" Mom brought her clasped hands to her chest.

"It's over, Mom."

CHAPTER 19

T HE STANDOFF BETWEEN Tristan and Casanova
continued. Matt, Silas, and Quinn appeared
on the horizon. Matt rode Gypsy, and my heart
pinched. Trout rode into view with Tristan's
brother, Justin, not far behind, sitting tall on his
dapple beauty.

Casanova's muscles spasmed, his ears pinned
back above a nervous glare.

Dad watched with a troubled gaze. Maggie,
between Dad and me, stroked Breeze's speckled
hindquarters. I stuck my fingers in my mouth and
blasted a quick, sharp whistle. Matt rode over.

"Would you mind escorting this guy back to
the truck? Could you take the key from the
ignition? Last thing I need to be is stranded." I
looked at my mom. "And when you do, please
check for snakes in the cab. The doors are open." I
handed Sands his broken phone.

Matt nodded. When Sands was back in the
truck bed, I turned my attention to Tristan, who
took slow strides toward the frazzled horse with a

lead rope in hand.

Maggie placed her hand on my arm. "I'm proud of you," she whispered.

"Me too, sweetheart. Glad your phone was working," Dad said.

"It wasn't. I wanted Mom and Mr. Sands to think it was. I'll call when I get back to the house." I handed Maggie the radio. "Can you listen for Glad, please?"

"Sure thing."

"Mom, I have business to tend to. You have less than a minute to explain."

"I thought a show would be something we could do together. I'd find a place here. You could use the money to renovate or expand, take care of those homeless horses your dad says you like to collect. There's an opportunity here."

"*Enough* with the opportunities." I planted my hands on my hips. "Isn't just being together enough?"

Sands sat on the wheel well and fiddled with his ruined phone. I didn't feel sorry for belting him, and I didn't regret smashing his phone. His greed to exploit my Montana home hadn't gotten him far.

"Chloe—" Mom rubbed her temples.

"This is part of your minute."

"I took down the nanny ads."

"Why would you do that?"

"Because I thought if you didn't find a nanny, you'd ask me to stay on. That was before Jeffrey was interested in the show. I just wanted to be part of your world." She frowned.

"You were part of my world. I can't believe you thought you needed to manipulate my life to be accepted. It doesn't work that way, Mom." Her minute was up.

Tristan's stance anchored the scene. He claimed the boundaries the open field lacked. Casanova eyed him, and Tristan met his horse's uneasy energy head-on. He clipped the lead to Casanova's bridle.

Tristan's gift took me from the hideousness of this moment as he and Casanova worked to establish common ground. Casanova was the horse Tristan boasted about. This was the horse that was going to beat my Gypsy.

"I'm sorry, Dad." My father shifted his weight and wiped his brow with the cloth from his pocket. Disappointing him always left me feeling shaky and like I should've known better. "I really thought Mom and I were getting somewhere. I trusted her."

"No need to apologize when it comes to matters of the heart," he said.

Goose bumps covered my arms, and I held his stare. His dark gaze flickered.

"You sound like Trout."

"I'll take that compliment, sweetheart."

I wrapped my fingers around his, and he squeezed my hand.

Mom's hidden agenda was now clear. Her ambition had shattered everything I let myself believe in—including my heart.

The lesson before me beckoned. Casanova's spirit rivaled my mother's. If I couldn't tame my mother, I'd take a crack at Casanova. The breeze swept across my cheeks like one of Grandpa's sweet kisses. I glanced toward the ridge marked with a stone cross and yellow rosebush in remembrance of him.

"Chloe—" Mom called.

"If she didn't feel strong enough, she wouldn't go. From where I sit, she'll be all right. Leave her be," Dad said.

With Tristan's approval, I walked across the field toward him and his unpredictable horse. The prospect of dealing with the creature consumed me. Casanova's Appaloosa roots were evident in his spotted hindquarters and independence. His dark chest glistened from work and tension.

Tristan's sweaty brow and intensity equaled the testy steed. Their rough exteriors were a mere reflection of troubled pasts.

Tristan held Casanova's attention steady with soft words and methodical movement, a language all their own. I wanted Tristan to teach me his ways.

The hard lines of Casanova's muscles were rigid with caution.

"Stand next to me, Chloe. It's okay, boy." Tristan's voice was deep and calm.

I did as Tristan said.

"Put your hand on my shoulder. You're a fool-headed woman for being out here, but I understand. I'm gonna hand you the lead. Today, Casanova and I are working on respect."

"We all are," I whispered, hoping the breeze's kiss upon my nape gave me the strength I needed to move forward.

"Do as I say," Tristan instructed.

I nodded.

"Now put your hand on mine," he said. "Fear has no place here."

Tristan's dusty skin was warm and rough. I swallowed trepidation and shook off nerves I didn't know existed. The spectators faded, and Tristan slipped the lead rope into my palm.

"I'm never afraid." My words were untrue but necessary. I didn't fear the land, wildlife, or the unknown. It was the fear of rejection I buried beneath a façade of denim, leather, and the brim of a cowboy hat.

As Tristan crept toward Casanova, he jerked his head with a whinny. The muscles in my hand knotted with the pressure of holding the rope, and I forced myself to loosen my grip. Respect was Tristan's word. I mimicked Tristan's movements and held Casanova's dark stare. Tristan ran his hand over Casanova's shoulder, not breaking his touch, walked in front of his horse to the other side, then tightened the girth. Casanova pawed at the ground. Clouds of dust blanketed his hooves.

"No one's here to hurt you," I said. "If they do, they'll have to answer to me, and nobody wants that. Just ask Jeffrey Sands."

Tristan peered over the saddle. I dug into my pocket and produced two sugar cubes. Tristan's brow creased with question.

"Did you hurt our Tristan?" With a secure lead, my intention was clear. I tugged downward on the lead just as I had seen Tristan do many times while working with Casanova in the pasture. "Good boy," I said. "You can have these if you want them."

I showed him the sugar. His snout fluttered with interest before eating it. I took more from my pocket.

"You're gonna lay down." There was a shift in his energy and stance. Receptive to the cue, he kneeled, then laid down. I stroked his neck, then rubbed his shoulder in large sweeping circles.

Casanova's breaths slowed, and his will drained into the earth.

"Here." I handed Tristan the sugar.

Tristan held the treat close to Casanova's nose. Gentle, purr-like breaths gave me goose bumps. Casanova lifted his head and took the sugar.

I crouched beside Casanova, staying clear of his hooves. "You're a handsome boy." Casanova lowered his head to the ground. "You gonna ride him, or are you done for the day? Dad has his medical bag if you need it."

"I'm riding," Tristan answered.

"I didn't expect anything less."

Tristan straddled his Appaloosa beauty. He put his boot in the free stirrup. With one hand, he stroked Casanova's sweaty hide. With the other hand, he held the horn of the saddle.

"You're a good boy, Casanova. Tristan's a good man."

Casanova found his balance on all fours with Tristan's cue.

"Should I unhook the lead or leave it on?"

"Unhook it."

I removed the lead. "I know how you're feeling, boy. It happens to the best of us." I produced more sugar, and he ate it.

I crept back to my father's side.

Tristan nudged Casanova forward. Casanova's front legs left the ground. His mane slashed the air when he reared up. Tristan took in the shock of the movement, unwilling to relent. Casanova's burst of energy was clearly his way of getting in the last word before settling down. Tristan tugged at the brim of his cowboy hat, then he and Casanova rode away.

"I can't believe what you two just did," Maggie said.

"I wonder if it works on people." I resisted the urge to glance at my mother. "Tristan said he wasn't hurt. Guess the medical bag goes home with me."

"See you back at the ranch." Dad coaxed Breeze into a full canter.

Matt and Justin rode over.

"You men did some great work out there," I said.

"We got all the strays. Thanks to this guy." Matt gestured to Justin, who wore an infectious grin.

"Nothing like a little chaos to keep you on your toes," I said.

"Wouldn't miss it for the world." Justin's cowboy posture softened as he took in the landscape. "This never gets old."

I glanced at Matt. "You and Gypsy seem to be getting along." Gypsy showed me her teeth. "I don't have any more sugar."

Matt pulled some from his pocket. He tossed it to me, and I fed it to her.

"Who's the guy in the truck?" Matt asked.

"Let's just say Mom's visit has turned into a Hollywood stunt that's not going to be a blockbuster hit. Mr. Sands is a producer. Apparently, they thought making our home into a reality show would make for profitable television."

"What?" Justin scratched his chin, then tugged the brim of his hat tight across his brow. "I bet you had something to say about that."

"I sure did. No doubt you'll hear about my behavior when you get back to the barn."

My mother lowered her gaze, walked back to the truck, and buckled up without saying a word to anyone.

I SAT ON the deck in my Adirondack chair, watching the sky. The setting sun hung low, and Lola was curled up at my feet. Lil had nursed, and I waited for Gracie to ring the dinner bell. The shuffle of Matt's boots drew me from my thoughts.

"What's going on, cowboy?"

"Did you *really* belt Mr. Sands?"

"Yup. I thought he was an intruder." I flexed my fingers. "Between that and Casanova, I'll be sore for a couple days. Casanova was worth it though."

"You've had a long day."

"He had it coming."

"That's my girl." Matt sat in the other Adirondack chair. "Your dad said you smashed Sands's phone."

"Yup, did that, too. Mom didn't say a word on the way back to the house."

"She's got some kooky ideas in that pretty head of hers."

"You think she's pretty?"

"Well, yeah. In a California glam sort of way. She's no Montana babe like you. By the way, where is she?"

"She drove into Bozeman with Sands. She took down the nanny postings, thinking if we didn't have one, I'd need her to stay." I scrutinized Matt's furrowed brow. "I trusted her. All she needed to do was talk to me. Everything just unraveled, and that Jeffrey Sands is just along for the ride. All he sees are dollar signs."

Matt put his hands behind his head and propped his feet up on the railing.

I braced myself at the sound of Gracie's whimpering cries. "After I get her down, maybe I can take a breather."

"That'd be nice. You're in high gear as usual. You know, this ranch isn't going anywhere."

I pushed myself up and shook out my legs. "Maggie tells me the girls will be grown before I know it."

"Most likely." Matt's eyes reflected the setting sun.

Gracie's cries subsided. With my hand on the door handle, I waited. When her soft whimpers didn't continue, I sat back down.

"We'll find a nanny without your mom. I'm heading to the barn to help Justin clean up. We have some catching up to do. Call me if you need to."

"Nice work with Gypsy today."

"She's up for the race," he said.

"Can't wait." I smiled and pictured myself in Grandpa's saddle, hunched low, feeling Gypsy's belly with the heels of my boots.

"We'll have to make a day of it—pig roast, beer, huckleberry pie, all the good stuff. Maybe even a trophy."

"I like the sound of that." I ran my fingers through my hair.

"What you and Tristan did today was impressive."

"It was mostly Tristan. He's a horse whisperer."

"So is someone else I know, and she's sitting next to me."

"I'm not sure that bribing animals with treats qualifies."

"It's more than that. The calves had to be creative to find their way back to this house. We'd fix one place in the fence, and they'd find another area to sabotage. They seem happier in the pen closer to you."

"I love these animals."

Matt patted my hand. The hint of electricity rippled between us.

"I'd better get going. Justin's gonna wonder where I am." Matt put his hat back on. "See you at dinner. I'll come by and help with the girls."

"Thanks." I took Matt's hand, and he pulled me up. "If you see my mom and Jeffrey Sands lurking about, let me know. Get your chores done and come home. We'll have dinner and put our feet up between the ballads of crying."

"I'd also like to steal some kisses." Matt put his arms around me.

"Isn't Justin waiting for you?"

"I'll let you go in a second." His gaze smoldered. "If your mom leaves, I'm ready to move in. Think about it, cowgirl."

He skipped down the deck stairs and sauntered away with a pep in his step, kicking up Montana dust, whistling as he went. I went inside and shut the door behind me. Shaking my head, I hustled into the living room. Glad was sitting on the sofa with Gracie.

"I'll take her, Gladiola."

"Gracie and I had a nice chat. She's not much of a talker. I'm going back to the main house to get you some dinner." Glad straightened her denim shirt.

"You don't have to do that." I propped myself up in the corner of the sofa with my favorite pillow behind my back.

"I know. I thought you and Matt would like some alone time. There's sloppy joe meat in the slow cooker. Enough for everyone."

"So—do you think my mom is coming back?"

"I'm not usually a betting woman, but I'd have

to say no. I'm sorry." Glad wrung her hands. "Maggie and I made lemon meringue pie. You could join us for dessert."

I draped a baby blanket over my shoulder to nurse Gracie, and Glad disappeared into the kitchen. She rummaged through the cupboards, doing Lord knew what. The sounds of drawers and dishes brought thoughts of Ida May cooking for her family after a hard day's work. Gracie nodded off, and I fixed my shirt. Before I could burp her, she spit up.

"Like you couldn't have waited a few seconds to do that on the burp cloth." She wiggled and squirmed as I called to Glad. "Fine, you win. I'm not sure I'll ever get used to that smell. Stinky."

"She got you, huh?" Glad wiped off my pants with a dish towel. "I set the table for you."

"Thanks. That's very sweet."

"I can snuggle with this little one while you change."

I put Gracie in Glad's arms.

"Sounds like number two is awake." Soft whimpers came from Lil's bassinet. Her pink cheeks bulged as if she were holding her breath. I wrapped her in the cotton blanket and picked her up.

"Maggie used to be quite the belcher, too."

Glad caressed Gracie's cheek. "Such a peanut. Soon you'll be a big girl."

Lola followed Lil and me upstairs. Glad followed with Gracie. I laid Lil in the middle of my bed and put a pillow on each side of her. Glad set Gracie on the bed, and we boxed her in too. Lola jumped up, circled them, and laid at their feet.

"I'll see you after dinner." Glad blew kisses to the girls and left.

"If I'm not there, the three of us have conked out."

I found a cottony summer dress I hadn't worn in ages in the closet. The stretchy, free-flowing material would fit nicely over my post-baby bump.

I kicked off my jeans, wiggled out of my tee, then slipped on the dress and tied the slender straps behind my neck. I inspected myself in the mirror and pushed away thoughts of my mother and her fashion advice.

I sat with the girls on the bed and stroked Lola's fur. I held out my finger, and Lil grabbed it. "Don't let go, little girl. Don't ever let go."

My mother had let me go a long time ago. Today's charade proved it.

CHAPTER 20

M ATT AND I had finished dinner. He did the dishes while I fed the girls. Mom hadn't called or returned to the ranch. She promised me eight weeks, and I was left with another visit cut short by a business deal. Her workaholic habits got the best of her, and I'd come in second. Once again, she'd given me up.

"I'll be outside when you're ready," Matt called from the kitchen.

"We're ready for dessert now." I buckled the girls into their seats, then slipped into my worn-out boots and fluffed my hair.

"Wow, you look great. The dress. The boots. The jacket."

My cheeks warmed at the compliment. "I thought I'd give the jeans and the bandanna a break."

"What happened to the studded boots?"

"I cleaned them up, put 'em back in the box, and tucked them away."

The walk to the main house was a one-sided

conversation. I talked. Matt listened and did a lot of whisker scratching. Dad waited for us on the front porch of the main house.

"Have you seen Mom?"

"Not since she drove off with that Sands fella. Looked like they were having words prior to getting into their cars," Dad answered.

"I'm *not* sorry for my behavior today."

"I'm not either. Family first makes for a true motto," Dad said. "Let's go inside."

The flawless view of the dusky Montana landscape filled the picture window in the living room. I took Lil from her carrier and handed her to Dad. A spark of light chased his disgruntled mood away. Being with family was the perfect ending to an otherwise lousy day.

Everyone was seated in the dining room. Maggie beamed when she noticed Dad holding Lil. "Hello, little one. You're sweet as can be," she said.

"I think she looks like Matt," I said.

Dad shrugged. "Hard to tell without the whiskers and the chaps."

"You're not gonna have whiskers. Don't let him tease you." Maggie caressed Lil's tiny fingers.

Matt sat with Gracie at the other end of the table. Glad swooned over them and cut Matt's pie into bite-sized pieces for him.

"That's quite the service, Gladiola." I counted the blessings before me, even if they didn't include my mother. Maggie cut me a slice of pie. I savored the towering meringue and lemon curd.

"Gracie's got a crush on her daddy. Look at those eyes. They'll be green as Irish fields," Glad said.

Tristan, Justin, Quinn, Silas, and Trout came in through the kitchen with a clamor. "You fellas sure do clean up nice," I said.

"Want me to hold Lil?" Maggie opened her arms.

"I got her. If all my pediatric patients had had her demeanor, I might have worked longer." Dad kissed her forehead.

"Definitely all Matt," Justin teased.

"I'm not sure I remember Chloe being this content," Dad said.

Gracie pressed her lips together, and her face turned bright red. Her tiny fingers balled into fists, her high-pitched scream shrill as an opera singer hitting high C.

"Now that—sounds familiar," Dad added.

"Thanks, Dad."

"No problem, sweetheart."

Matt slid his chair back from the table and left

the room to console her.

"What do you suppose Mom and Mr. Sands are doing in Bozeman? Do you think they got on a plane and left?"

Dad sipped his coffee and fiddled with his napkin, his interest in my mother nil. Trout sipped his coffee, too, then set the cup on the saucer. His hard gaze met my father's. The exchange between the two men heeded no explanations. The chatter ceased.

"I spoke to Mr. Putnam, filled him in on the day's events, and made it clear we weren't interested in a contract for a reality television show. I found Sands's contact information online and gave it to Mr. Putnam. Putnam said he'll take care of it. I don't think we'll be seeing or hearing from Mr. Sands again." I met each spectator's gaze. "Did I do something wrong?"

"Quite the contrary. You met the oncoming train head-on, and we all know that wasn't easy for you," Dad said.

Maggie raised her glass and toasted me. Everyone followed suit, then Dad whispered to Lil.

"I hope you're not telling her secrets about me," I said.

"Hardly. Nursery rhymes and warnings about your temper and work ethic. You did my momma and your granddaddy proud today."

"My turn to hold her. You've had her long enough." Maggie straightened Lil's blanket, then took her from Dad.

"This is going to bode well living around a bunch of people enamored with babies. I'm sorry Mom opted out. Silas, do you want a turn?"

"Sure would. Right after I have seconds."

"We'll discuss your mother later. It's family time," Dad said.

When Gracie stopped screaming, she and Matt returned to the table.

"May I?" Tristan's question stopped the conversation.

"Really?" Matt asked.

"Yes. I may be able to rival Silas's charm," Tristan answered.

"I'll believe it when I see it," Silas joked.

"You won't pull any of those horse whispering moves on her, will you?" I reciprocated Tristan's crooked grin.

"Would that be so bad? There might be less crying if I did." Gracie fussed. "Now, now, little girl. You ain't no different from Casanova. I can see it in your eyes. Your daddy is gonna have to keep an eye on you." Tristan rocked Gracie in his arms. She yawned, then nodded off.

"Amazing. Do you make house calls? Let's say around 3:00 a.m.?" I responded before anyone else could speak. "I don't believe it. She's yours. Silas, I'll need you for backup."

Matt laughed and ate the rest of his pie.

Glad's gaze met Tristan's. "She's not kidding. She *will* call you."

"A family is more than blood," I said to Tristan. "Equity and fair opportunity make for happy kin."

"You've done it, boy. There isn't any escaping now." Trout sipped his coffee and peered at Tristan over the rim of the cup. "True story, and I have no intention of cutting ties." The apples of his cheeks held a smile. "You're growing a mighty big family here, John McIntyre."

"Sure am." Dad's pride shone at the corners of his eyes. "Soon, we'll need a bigger table."

Matt squeezed my knee. Tristan handed Gracie to Glad. "You two feel like taking a little walk?" she asked. "We'll keep an eye on the babies."

"Better get while the getting is good. Never know when you might get the chance again. Babies are a tricky commodity." Dad sipped his coffee.

"We won't be long. There's something I want to show you." I tugged at Matt's hand and scooted my chair away from the table.

"All right then. We'll be back shortly."

"Maggie, can I borrow a warmer jacket?" I asked.

"There's plenty to choose from in the mud-room."

"Go before the girls start in again." Dad shooed us away.

Matt and I scurried through the kitchen and out the back door after grabbing Maggie's corduroy barn coat. Matt took my hand, jerked me backward, and I landed in his arms. His lips grazed mine.

"You should wear dresses more often," he whispered.

"We'll see."

"So stubborn." Matt rested his hands on the small of my back. "What's out here that I need to see?"

"I was up in the loft of the old barn earlier. Come on." I intertwined my fingers with his. We strolled past 311 and 313's pen. They came to the fence and stuck their ebony noses through the rails. "Hi, girls." Calf 311 nudged my belly. "No more babies," I told her.

Gypsy glanced at me from the corral and let out a sweet sigh. Her heavy eyelids gave way to the evening. The sky twinkled with stars, and I was sure we were getting closer to heaven with each passing day.

I unlatched the hook on the old barn door and slid it open. A lantern sat on the tack box. I turned it on, and the glow of the warm light brought the old barn to life. I beckoned Matt to follow me upstairs to the loft. He turned on the bare bulb hanging overhead in the center of the room.

"Looks cleaner and bigger than the day I moved the furniture to the house with the guys," he said.

I held his hand. "I swept. Threw some things away. I think it's time we make this space useful again."

For a moment, the world was silent, and I saw Grandpa and Ida May slow dancing at the opposite end of the loft. I took in their smiles before they disappeared.

"What is it?" Matt squeezed my hand.

"I saw Grandpa and Ida May." I pointed toward the window at the far end of the loft.

"They can't spend all their time on the ridge." He turned off the overhead light.

I put my finger to my lips.

"Listen. The silence is bliss." I moved closer to where I'd seen my grandparents. Matt followed, set his lantern on the floor, slipped his arm around me, and led me in a dance of our own. My cheeks warmed. A tingle trickled down my spine as I leaned into him.

"Keep dancing, cowboy." The hem of my dress brushed the back of my knees as I followed his lead.

"Where do you think my mom went?"

"I'm sure we'll find out soon enough." He held my stare. "Let's finish this dance."

I settled back into his body, his whiskers rough against my cheek. When the dance ended, Matt kissed me.

"That was nice," I whispered.

Matt turned off the lantern, and we gazed out the window at the sleepy 617 Ranch. Light glowed from the houses. I pressed the palm of my hand against the glass.

"Isn't it beautiful?"

"Sure is. You've had quite the day. Are you tired?" Matt put his arm around my waist.

"No. Today was an answer. Maybe not the answer my heart wanted, but I know where I stand with my mother. Sands wasn't the only loser. I have to move on."

"I'm proud of you. The bunkhouse will be chatty tonight."

Whispers drifted between us until his lips met mine.

"Chloe. Someone is downstairs."

We tiptoed across the floor, kneeled, and listened. I held up two fingers.

Matt crouched beside me. "Who is it?"

I shrugged.

"Why are we whispering? This is silly. Last time you didn't ask, someone ended up with a bloody nose."

I turned on my lantern and motioned for him to follow me. There was no one at the bottom of the stairs. Matt took the lantern, then inspected the nooks and unlit crannies.

"I heard footsteps," he said. "Winston and Ida May?"

I smiled, turned off the lantern, and set it back on the tack box with a nod.

Twinkle stars lit the night sky. I wished upon them like I did every night. I didn't wish for my mother's return. Instead, I wished her a happy life and strength to move on, too.

Matt and I closed the barn door, then strolled back along the gravel road to the main house.

Dad sipped a glass of warm milk in the kitchen. Samson paced at his feet.

"The girls are back at your house with Maggie and Glad."

"Thanks, Dad. I'll see you tomorrow." I

hugged him. He was my rock.

"Night, sweetheart. We'll start over in the morning."

"I know. See you at dawn." I scratched Samson's back before leaving.

"Chloe—"

"Yeah, Dad."

"If you need to talk about your mother, you know where to find me. It's never easy to see your children disappointed."

"I'll be fine." Truth was, I didn't know how long it would take to just be *fine*. I held the silver heart hanging around my neck; the edges dug into the palm of my hand.

Matt walked me home. We stood outside, gazing at the timber house, its windows lit with warm light and a sense of peace.

Matt and I took our boots off in the mudroom. Thoughts of a prairie girl in a log cabin with her family and dog drifted through my mind as a coyote's howl echoed in the distance. The boxed set of books telling the stories of the little house in the big woods were packed away and stored at the back of my closet, next to the boots my mother had given me.

Maggie and Glad were huddled on the sofa, Glad beneath a fleecy throw blanket.

"She's all yours," Matt said before kissing my cheek. "If you need me, you know where to find me."

"Thanks, Matt. Good night." I sat on the ottoman and waited for the back door to shut. I wiped the tears from the corners of my eyes. Maggie scooted over and patted the cushion between her and Glad. I accepted the invite, rested my head on her shoulder, and cried.

CHAPTER 21

MOM HAD LEFT a week ago. The twins and I had gotten into a routine without her. When they were hungry, I fed them. When diapers needed changing, I changed them. When Matt was around, I let him have a turn. It didn't seem right to hog the experience. When the girls slept, I rested. I researched nanny services, handled paperwork, did laundry, skimmed photos— anything to keep me busy and my mind free of you-know-who.

When Gracie and Lil cried, I consoled them. The life-sized stuffed ponies in the girls' room were draped with onesies, mismatched socks, and cushy blankets I wanted to snuggle with.

I'd answered calls regarding the nanny position. No one seemed good enough, and I cursed my mom for leaving, because she had been a nanny I would have hired. She sang, read, held the girls, doted on them in a way I don't remember her doting on me.

When it came time to clean out the guest room,

I planned to triage, purge, and leave the past where it belonged—behind me. There would be no lingering of any kind. I opened the door, raised the blinds with a startling clack, and stared at the odds and ends my mother had left behind.

I put the lighter of the two suitcases from the closet on the bed, packed the random art supplies from the desk, two blank sketchbooks, and a book of fabric swatches I hadn't seen before. I tossed in the perfume she left on the nightstand last, zipped it up, and set it in the corner. I stripped the bed, ripped off the dust ruffle and tossed it on the heap of linens. I whacked my toe on the bedframe and fell to the floor in a crumpled heap.

Lying in the pile of snow-white linens, I swished my arms and legs, hoping to see the impression of an angel when I stood. Angels made everything better. The two napping angels across the hall were living proof. My hand hit something beneath the bed, and I rolled onto my stomach to see an olive green leather journal filled with pictures of me from birth until now, except for a faded color photo taped to a pink notecard. I couldn't read the smudged date. The man and woman holding hands wore jeans, leather vests, and cowboy hats, her beaded belt buckle like a design I'd seen in Mom's up-and-coming collection.

I got up, set Mom's journal on the desk before getting the second suitcase from the closet and unzipping it. I unpacked the gift boxes tied with ribbon and set them on the bed. I opened the card.

Dear Chloe,

For you. You said no more gifts, and sticking to your wishes was hard. These blouses are a thank-you that I simply left behind to remind you how special you are. The belt is a piece Hermione designed. The design represents sacred power and life. This piece is more than purposeful design—it's a testimony to inner strength.

All my love,
Coco

I opened the boxes. She'd included the white blouse with the slubby stitching I liked and five others I hadn't seen in the magazine. I fingered the multicolored beaded belt in the last box, then wrapped it around my waist. I had to shed a few more pounds before I'd be able to wear it comfortably. There wasn't one blouse it didn't compliment. The hues of green, yellow, blue, and rose defined Mother Earth. I hung the blouses and the belt in the closet, put the suitcases away, and shut the closet door.

I took my phone from my back pocket and dialed her number. The call went straight to voicemail. "Hi, Mom. It's Chloe. Call me when you can."

I laid back down on the floor in the nest of bedding, waiting for a response. The scent of Mom's perfume would be washed away after a hot cycle and become a distant memory again. The magazine samples reminding me of her that I kept in my beat-up purple journal would not be wasted.

"Chloe, are you up here?" Trout's voice echoed in the hallway.

I didn't move. I closed my eyes. His footsteps grew louder. When I opened my eyes, he stood over me with his hands on his hips.

"What in tarnation are you doing on the floor?"

"Laundry. Why are you here?"

"Doesn't look like laundry, and checking on you. Everyone's out workin' except Glad. She sent me 'cause she hasn't seen or heard from you today. It's her baking day, and nothing takes her away from the kitchen on a Tuesday morning. She wants to know if you're still breathing."

"I'm fine. Just dandy." I forced a toothy smile. "Can you help me up?" I grabbed his hand and got to my feet. "I'm cleaning up my mother's things.

Check it out." I showed him the leather journal the color of a martini garnish and the pink notecard inside. "I can't believe my mom had dark hair. Look at those bell bottoms and vests. Wish it wasn't so blurry."

"Time does funny things to a memory." A shadow drifted over his stare. He placed the card in his shirt pocket and left without saying another word.

I called after him, "Wait. Where are you going? What's the matter? Trout. Come back here. Trout!"

I stood at the top of the staircase, waiting for him to return. My mother had caused yet another wake and she wasn't even here.

"You know I can't leave the babies! Come back here." I hurried downstairs behind him. The porch door at the front of the house clapped shut, and he was gone.

I SAT BEHIND the wheel of Grandpa's vintage truck, the knots in my belly from leaving the girls with Milly Thompson, a friend of Glad's from the Women's Club she'd joined. Milly's sunny disposition hadn't convinced me she could handle the twins for the day, but I was willing to give the arrangement a shot.

Getting out of the house was at the top of my to-do list, and Glad had made it happen with a few phone calls after Trout had reported back to her. I'd written out instructions and showed Milly how the two-way radio worked. She'd called me twice to tell me everything was cool back at the house. Even so, I worried.

Sooner than later, I'd be wrangling full-time and leaving the girls with a nanny would be old hat, but this first step proved harder than expected. I'd checked my radio multiple times, making sure the volume was loud enough and the battery hadn't died. The struggle was real. I'd compromise and check in midafternoon.

Matt and Dad rode in the distance. The clouds threatened rain, but the calmness on the horizon pacified my impulse to drive home. I got out of the truck to stretch my legs. Maggie rode across the field on Cora. I grabbed my camera from the front seat and snapped several pictures.

"Hey there," Maggie called.

"Hi. What brings you out?"

"Thought I'd take a break from organizing photos and get some fresh air."

I inspected my radio one more time, hooked it back on my belt, and patted Cora's snout.

"It's natural to worry. I stopped in before I left. Milly's doing a fine job handling the girls."

"Are the girls *really* okay?"

"Yes. Milly appears to be holding her own. The crying doesn't seem to faze her."

"Matt has more cattle coming in the spring. Twenty head. Pretty soon, this sea of white will be salt and pepper proper. He and Dad have a timetable for breeding the Black Angus and the White Park. Should be interesting. Matt says the meat will be premium."

"Go check on the girls. The guys will understand." Maggie dismounted Cora and dropped the reins in the grass. "You don't always need to be tough, Chloe. Changing your mind isn't a sign of weakness. Sometimes taking a step back eases the pressure and makes the picture clearer."

"Don't I know it." I turned off the camera. "Thanks for checking on Milly and the girls. What's Glad up to?"

"She finished baking and is in the garden with Samson."

"Digging holes?"

"No. He's leaving that to her." Maggie laughed.

"Will you tell Dad and Matt that I headed in for a bit? I'll catch up with them later."

"Sure thing. I'll be home shortly. That's if your dad doesn't put me to work. And Chloe—we have instincts for a reason."

I got back in the truck, waved goodbye, and drove away. The breeze filled the cab with sweet memories of me riding with Grandpa and Dad when I was a child. Sitting between them was the safest place in the world. Laughing at their jokes made me an equal even if I didn't understand the punchline, and they taught me how to drive when I was old enough to see over the dashboard.

The truck bumped along. Rain dripped on the windshield in a lazy wave, then stopped. I lifted my chin to the open road and enjoyed the ride. "You know, Ida May, I didn't get the short end of the stick after all. Those two waiting for me at home are a blessing. I would've missed them every day had they not chosen me to be their momma." I glanced at the empty passenger seat. "Gracie May, Lil, and I will have memorable adventures in this truck."

Back home, I parked under the shade tree next to a jeep I didn't recognize. Milly had opened the windows, and Grandma's lace curtains billowed in the breeze on the first floor. The unusual quiet pricked my nerves. A young woman in a navy floral dress and cowboy boots met me on the porch.

"Hi there. Can I help you?" I asked.

"Hi." Her voice trembled as she tucked her short brown hair behind her ears.

"Are you okay? You seem a bit out of sorts."

"I am. When I got here, the babies were crying, and no one answered the door. So I went in."

I ran inside. The young woman followed.

"Milly. Milly!" My frantic call was met with silence.

"She's upstairs with the babies. Everything is okay now," the young woman said.

"Who are you? And what do you mean, everything is okay?"

Milly came downstairs. "Thank you again for your help." She turned her attention to me. "I was so busy with the girls, I didn't eat. Good thing this young lady wasn't shy about investigating the fuss. The girls were crying, and I was too shaky to move, and I'd left the radio upstairs. I should've made time to eat."

"My dad is in the field. If you need medical attention, I'm sure he'd come in. He's a retired pediatrician and our go-to guy when someone's sick or needs stitches." I took the radio from my belt. "Please. Sit down." I helped Milly to the sofa.

"This young lady handled the babies with such care and made me a snack. Gracie and Lil are sound asleep in their cribs."

I turned to the young woman. "Why are you here, again?"

"I received a call this morning from the Rock-A-Bye Baby agency you listed the nanny position with. I'd applied before and thought the job was filled because it had been taken down. Anyway, a woman named Coco called and asked me to come out for an interview. She said she'd notified you. Obviously, that's not the case. I apologize for coming in unannounced."

"What did you say your name was?"

"I'm Maria Santos. I can see the position is filled, so I'll leave you ladies. It was nice meeting you. Glad I could help." She turned to leave.

"The position isn't filled."

Maria turned on a boot heel with a budding smile.

"Milly's only doing me a favor for the day. I appreciate you stepping in. I'm Chloe McIntyre. Pleased to meet you." I shook her hand.

"Thank goodness you showed up." Milly pulled a linen hankie from her sleeve and fingered the scalloped edges. "The last time my sugar took a dip, I passed out and spent the night in the hospital. Maria knew exactly what to do."

"My mother has hypoglycemia, too. I would've

called for help if the snack didn't work. You sure you're okay?" She sat on the ottoman and doted on Milly.

"I'm feeling much better. Thank you," Milly said.

"You should eat," I replied.

"You sure you don't mind?"

"Please. I'd have to answer to Glad if something happens to you."

Milly's chins jiggled with laughter, and her cheeks became rosy. "My lunch is in the refrigerator. I packed a turkey sandwich and a peach."

"I'll get it so Ms. McIntyre can check on the girls." Maria went into the kitchen.

"That girl's an angel. You're a fool if you don't hire her," Milly whispered.

I smiled and went upstairs. The girls had been changed into fresh outfits and were sound asleep. I stood in their room, remembering Mom's voice when she sang to them. As much as I wanted to hold them, I resisted. I'd learned early on never to wake a sleeping baby.

I went back downstairs, ran my fingers over the silver horseshoes tacked to the mantel, and peeked into the kitchen. Maria and Milly sat at the table, swapping stories about babysitting. My mother hadn't sent me an extravagant gift to make up—

she'd sent something she knew Gracie May and Lil needed.

"Tell me about your family," Milly said before taking a bite of her sandwich. "I have two grown girls, twenty-eight and twenty-two."

"I live with my mom."

I stepped into the kitchen and poured myself a glass of ice water. "I didn't mean to interrupt. I'd like to hear about your family, too. Would you like a cold drink?"

"Water, please."

"You got it."

"Well—I came home from college to help my mom care for my dad when his lung cancer spread. He's been gone almost four months." The corners of her mouth drew down. "I decided it was time to get back to work. I'd like to finish my early education degree someday, but it's not time. I should stay close to home for my mom. I really like the daycare center and the families I work with."

"If you already have a job you like, why'd you come out?" I asked.

Maria glanced away.

"Go on, tell her," Milly said, brushing the crumbs from her shirt.

"The woman who called told me about the ranch, and I had to see it for myself. She said you'd be a fantastic boss, and your twins were angels. The pay beats the daycare center's." She swirled the water around in her glass. "She mentioned you had horses."

"Horses do have a draw. Do you have one?"

"Two. Xena and Cookie, and they need homes. My mom's selling the farm, and I won't have anywhere to keep them."

"Ah," I said, lifting my chin. "Did the woman on the phone happen to mention that I have a soft spot for homeless animals?"

Maria lowered her gaze. "I'm not here just because of the horses. Thinking you'd let me board them is a fantasy, but I couldn't *not* ask. Day-dreaming about keeping my horses consumes me. Even if they can't stay here, I'd really like the job. I saw the herd when I drove in." She rubbed her forearms. "Gives me goose bumps."

Milly's pleading expression tugged at my heart.

"I told the woman I work for that I might be leaving. She knows I'm here."

"Would her name be Coco by any chance?"

"No, her name is Amy Brentwood, and she's looking for a replacement at the daycare center as we speak."

"Could you write down Amy's number? I'll give her a call." I handed Maria a notepad and a pencil.

"I'm sure there's more you'd like to know about me. Ask me anything. You people sure are nice." She jotted Amy's number down along with the daycare center's name.

"Did Coco happen to get your background information when she called?"

"I'm not sure what you're referring to, but she did ask me a lot of questions."

"I figured. She's thorough." I sipped my water. "How do you feel about family dinners?"

"My mom insists on them. No phones though." She shook a scolding finger. "I didn't always appreciate family dinners growing up, but I sure do miss them now that my dad's gone. I learned a lot listening to my parents. The dinner table was where I got to know them. Really know them. You know what I mean?"

"I do," I answered.

"Did I mention I can start dinner for you and that I do laundry?"

"Could you excuse me for a minute? I'd like to peek in on the girls again. I'll be back in a minute." I walked out of the kitchen and put Amy's number in my phone before it left my mind. I went upstairs, peeked in on the girls, and called Maria's boss.

"Buckaroos and Little Ladies Too Daycare.

This is Amy Brentwood."

"Hi there. My name is Chloe McIntyre. Maria Santos is interviewing for the nanny position I have available, and I was wandering if you could tell me about her."

"Oh darn," Amy said.

"I beg your pardon."

"Excuse me. Maria mentioned the interview today. I was hoping she wouldn't be a good match, for selfish reasons. She's the best caregiver I have, and the kids love her. When the center is closed, she babysits for my clients on the side. If she leaves, little Jack is going to be heartbroken. He's four and has quite the crush on her. I knew someone would snatch her up. She says you've got land and animals. That girl loves the outdoors as much as she loves children."

"I see. I wish I could tell you she isn't a good fit. When she got here today, the sitter was having a medical issue, and Maria stepped in, a lifesaver. If she needs to stay on until you find someone, I understand."

"If you could hold out a week, I'd be grateful. It wouldn't be fair of me to keep her any longer. Her mother's downsizing. She understands why her mom has to sell the family farm, but saying goodbye to a childhood home is like losing another part of you. If she loses those horses, too, she'll be crushed."

"I appreciate your kindness, Amy. May I call if I have any other questions?"

"Sure thing. Hope it works out," Amy said before ending the call.

Milly and Maria were still chatting at the kitchen table when I returned.

"Is everything okay, dear?" Milly asked.

"Milly, would you mind if I talked to Maria outside?"

"Sure, dear."

Maria and I walked through the living room. I held the front door to the front porch open for her, then followed her outside. "Maria, I called your boss at the daycare. She says the children really like you. I hear Jack will be a bit upset."

"I can't believe Miss Amy mentioned Jack. He's pretty attached." Maria blushed. "He likes older women."

"I can't agree to take your horses on until I speak with my dad. You see, I've taken in my fair share without telling him."

"I understand."

"Do you have the rest of the day off?"

"Yes, ma'am." She squared her shoulders.

"Ms. McIntyre is fine." I smiled. "Could you

stay? I'd like to show you the ropes. If we get a chance, I could introduce you to the horses."

"Sure." Her dark eyes sparkled.

"What I'm trying to say is, you've already proven yourself, but I'd like to get to know you better before I offer you the job. I want you to make sure this job suits you." My chest rose and fell with a sigh of hope. "Family dinners are important around here, too. If you take the position, we'd expect you to stay from time to time."

"I'd like that."

"Me too."

CHAPTER 22

MARIA HAD SHOWN up on time every day, which was no less than ten minutes early, according to her. Lil and Grace took to her easily. She was a dream come true, and she hadn't been sent from heaven—she'd been sent by a blonde Hollywood bombshell attempting to repair our broken relationship.

With each passing week, I spent more time with the wranglers, easing back into the schedule I expected from myself. Leaving Gracie and Lil at the house tugged at my heartstrings, and I couldn't wait for them to grow into the sidekicks I imagined them to be.

Perched in my grandpa's saddle, I savored the sunrise. It was my first official, full day back to work as foreman, and I couldn't think of a better way to celebrate my twenty-seventh birthday than riding my Gypsy.

The horses stepped from the shadows of the trees, carrying the morning haze upon their backs. We had a good month of summer left, and I looked forward to riding up to Grandpa's ridge to tend the rosebush, checking on the cattle in the afternoons, and managing the wranglers I'd missed working alongside from sunup to sundown.

"My circle begins and ends with you, sweet Gypsy girl." I stroked her neck. The words on the scrap of paper I'd found in Trout's book had made a lasting impression. "Souls may come and go, but friendship and love remain constant. When we trip upon the hard times, it is nothing more than a way for destiny to propel us to a place we were meant to be." I stood in my stirrups and hugged my best girl. "It sure feels good to be back."

Matt trotted over on Trigger. "Hey there. I like that leather jacket, birthday girl."

I settled back into the saddle and took hold of the reins. "Thanks. Couldn't bring myself to buy new boots. Bought a jacket instead. I like the fringe and the way it slaps against the leather when I ride. A different kind of music."

"You ready to run these horses home? Silas's singing may be their wake-up call, but what they're really looking for is you."

Gypsy pawed at the ground, her twitching shoulder my signal to get down to business.

Tristan's voice came over the radio loud and clear. "You take the lead, bosslady. It's good to have you back."

I took the radio from my belt. "It's good to be here. I've missed y'all. Let's bring 'em home."

I secured the radio, clicked my tongue, and fell into the rhythm of Gypsy's canter like we'd never been apart. Thundering hooves nipped at her heels, and she slipped into a realm where nothing existed except the two of us, until the horses were safely corralled.

Maggie and Glad waited near the adjacent pasture with Maria and the girls. Maggie took pictures. Glad held a steaming cup of coffee, a fleecy scarf tied around her neck to ward off the morning chill. I dismounted Gypsy, tied her to the hitching post, and waved Maria over.

"I know that look," I said to her. "Go on, pet her."

Maria stroked Gypsy's hide, a longing in her eyes.

"We'll go for a ride soon. Thanks for being here."

"Thanks for hiring me." She leaned close as the wranglers rode in. "I can't believe you get to work with them every day. Brings back memories of riding with my dad." She lowered her voice. "I've got a soft spot for cowboys."

"Me too." I waved Matt over. "I think it's

time," I said to him.

"Time for what? Are you gonna start bossing me around already?"

I held on to Trigger's bridle. "I'm that predictable, huh?"

"Nah. What do you have in mind?"

"The girls and I are ready for you to move in. I'm on solid ground, and they'd like to see their daddy on a regular basis."

"Justin might have something to say about that." Matt knocked his hat back with a smile.

Justin sauntered over when he heard his name. "What would I have a say about?"

"I'm moving in with my girls."

Justin snatched his hat from his head, jumped, and kicked his heels together. "It's about time she reined you in."

"You just want the bigger room in the bunkhouse," Matt said.

"Heck yeah, I do."

My radio beeped, and I answered Trout's call. "What's going on?"

"Could you ride over? I'm at the cabin."

"Sure. Is everything all right?" I looked at Matt. He shrugged.

"I'll be there in a few." I ended the call and secured the radio to my belt. "Wonder what's going on." I untied Gypsy, climbed the mounting block, and saddled up. "Gonna take my favorite ride." I blew a kiss to the girls and circled around. "Hey, Maria. You still interested in bringing Xena and Cookie on board?"

She nodded, her smile as wide as the Grand Canyon.

"I've made a deal with my dad. I've got an appointment today with a guy who's interested in four of our mares. Once we sign the papers, you and I can discuss making the move."

"Thank you, ma'am." She stumbled over her words. "Sorry, I'm having a hard time calling you Ms. McIntyre."

"You know what?" I pushed my hat back. "Ma'am is just fine."

I TIED GYPSY to the hitching post outside Trout's cabin and went inside. He'd hung a pair of sun-bleached elk antlers above the fireplace since my last visit. The picture he'd put in his pocket and taken the day I'd packed my mother's things was propped up on the mantel.

"What's going on, cowboy?"

"How was the morning run, birthday girl?"

"Is this something I need to sit for? Matt and I

hired a nanny. You've been mighty scarce."

"You wearing a new jacket? Thought shopping wasn't your thing."

"You're not sick, are you? You look healthier than ever."

"You gonna stop asking questions anytime soon? You've always been a handful."

"You started it. Why am I here?"

"You speak to your mother recently?"

"I'll stand."

"Ain't nowhere to run, kid."

"I've been done running for a while now. I thought I made that clear."

"I'm just making sure." He scratched his bushy brow. "I like that beaded hatband. Reminds me of someone I knew a long time ago."

"I think I'll sit now. I see you put my parents' picture on the mantel."

"Chloe—I asked you a question."

"Must be a doozie if you're calling me by name."

Trout's chest rose and fell with a sigh. "You're not gonna go easy on me, are you?"

"That's up to you. You know you're my favorite. We've been together a long time, and I want to keep it that way."

"I'd like that, too." His moustache twitched.

"Did your mother ever explain the kiss?"

"Nope."

"You ever gonna ask me what happened? Consider the invite a birthday present."

"Nope. Donate that present to charity." I glanced around the living room. "Did you clean in here? Looks neater than usual."

"Your mother thought kissing me would prove a point. Not very flattering."

"I'm still not interested. I said I've let it go." I ran my fingertips along the bookshelves, checking for dust.

"The point's been moot for years but not forgotten."

"You becoming hard of hearing? I don't want to know."

"My past concerns both of us."

"This isn't much of a birthday present. What's behind door number two?"

"There ain't no door number two," he grunted.

"I stopped leaving Mom messages a while ago. She's been quiet since she left. You and I don't have any scars between us, and I hope there never are."

"Taking chances is part of life. And you'd be right smart to remember that when it comes to your daughters' daddy. He's a good man, doing the right thing."

"Thought this discussion was about you. Is it time for me to leave?"

"You can't escape hurt, kid. Whether it's a snake bite, a scrape from a fall, a broken nose from a feisty broad, or a woman who thinks she's gotta prove herself."

"Now we're getting somewhere." I took my hat off and set it on the sofa beside me. "Thought talking 'bout women was off-limits."

"Guess you forgot this conversation was a birthday present. Her name was Hermione Crow."

"Oh." Time stood still with the hitch in my breath. My mind reeled.

"Your momma thought she could get me to air my feelings."

"Well, that backfired," I said.

"I've been scarce for a reason."

"Scarce. Heck, you've been hiding out, and she hasn't been here for weeks."

"Sometimes a man needs time to think."

"You gonna get to the good part of this story soon?"

"Impatience is the road to regret." Trout clicked his tongue.

"Been there before. Suppose I'll be there again."

"At my age, I'll sidestep the opportunity. You'd be wise to think about following my lead. When Hermione and I said goodbye, I thought for sure she'd be back in a month. A month turned into three months, then a year. That year ain't ended yet."

"Sorry." His ache was mine. "What are you gonna do about it?"

"I rebuilt this family home. Now, it's time I rebuilt that relationship. Absence didn't make the heart grow fonder. Hell, I didn't even know I had a heart until I heard her voice again. Your momma is the reason she's returning."

"You're making me nervous. Who's return-ing?" I cleared my throat and tugged at my collar. "It's mighty warm in here."

"Hermione."

"I thought you meant my mother."

"I did." He lowered his gaze. "Just thought I'd give you a moment to breathe before I sucker punched you on your birthday."

"This is turning into some day." I fiddled with my hat. "I thought she and I were done."

"Are you? Are you willing to let her go? Clear the air. You don't want a never-ending year like the one I've had."

I made myself comfortable and propped my

feet up on the ottoman.

"Those boots are goners, kid. Suck it up and get new ones. What happened to the fancy pair?"

"The jacket is new. I like the fringe," I said. "When does the past stop mattering?"

"Not sure. For me, it was the day your mother—"

I threw my hands in the air. "Don't even say it. Does my dad know about Hermione? And Maggie?"

"You ain't gonna like my answer."

"I'm the last to know again." I sighed.

"Kid, you've got more distractions than a carnival. Think of it as common courtesy."

"Gee, thanks, I guess."

"Those aren't your parents in that picture. It's me and Hermione just before she left. That was a long time ago, and talking about age is still off the table." The dip in his brow was deep. "I was set on working with your granddaddy, and she had things to do. She knew it was time to fly, and I let her. I'm no city boy. I see you doing the math in your head. Don't."

I stood and took the photo from the mantel.

"It's time for you to complete the circle." My words weren't much louder than a whisper.

"I hope you liked the storybook as much as

Hermione's note inside."

"She gave that note to you?"

"Yes. The day she left."

"I'm not mad at you, Trout."

"Good thing. 'Cause I'm tired, kid."

"Me too."

"Twins will do that. Ain't nothing good comes from kissing a cowboy."

"Sometimes it does." I placed the photo back on the mantel. "Why did my mom have the picture?"

"Hermione gave it to her. You weren't supposed to see it."

"Remember that day at the pond before the babies came?"

"Yes, and I thought giving you that feather would make that pesky bird go away."

I chuckled. "I said the bird's gift was wisdom and if you remained open-minded, insight would come your way."

"The crow's message was meant for both of us."

"I'm not so sure I want to meet the woman who broke your heart."

"She didn't break my heart. That was my own doing when I let her walk away. We all make choices."

"When are they getting here?"

The sound of tires on the gravel drive answered me before he could.

I set the photo back on the mantel, then put my cowboy hat on.

Trout nodded, pushed himself up from the chair, and answered the door. Polite greetings were exchanged on the porch. I watched through the screen door as Trout kissed Hermione's cheek. Mom stood in the background, enjoying the reunion. I glanced down at my boots. The worn soles and faded leather had taken me more miles than I could count. It didn't seem right to rob them of one last adventure.

I shuffled out to the porch, unsure of how to act, what to say, what not to say, or how to even breathe.

"This is Chloe," Trout said, his gaze aglow.

I shook Hermione's hand. "Nice to meet you."

She took my hands in hers. "This pretty little thing is the one who broke Jeffrey's nose in two places?"

"Yes, ma'am, that was me."

Hermione gave me a big hug. I hugged her back even though I wasn't sure my arms worked. My gaze met my mother's over Hermione's shoulder. Mom wore faded denim, a white tee, and a shearling shawl I'd seen in her sketchbook.

"You're my hero. Sands is a slimeball," Hermione said.

Mom stepped up on the porch. "I know that now. He insisted on seeing the ranch. I didn't mean for things to spiral out of control. By the time the day was done, I was so embarrassed and ashamed for entertaining the idea that the ranch could bring us together in that way. I'm so sorry, Chloe."

I didn't know how to respond. I tucked my hands into my pockets and lowered my gaze.

"There are things we need to discuss," she said.

"Trout told me all I need to know. These boots don't have enough life in them to go backward."

"I still think we should talk." She pulled the journals I'd mailed to her from her purse.

"Glad the package I sent made it to your door."

She leafed through the pages. "These sketches don't belong to me. I can't take credit for work I didn't do."

"Not sure what you mean. I couldn't throw the journals away. I don't like waste. Not gonna lie, I had a moment with the scissors, and a sizable portion of the fabric swatches you left behind were sacrificed. Then one thing led to another and, well, what's left of your art supplies and fabric samples is in that book."

"I let Jeffrey talk me into something I knew was wrong."

"Maybe if you would've stayed, those sketches in your hand wouldn't have happened. Being creative helped me process our relationship. Kind of like therapy. And you were doing it with me even though you weren't here."

"Chloe, these designs are more than scribbles and salvaged swatches of cloth. They're proof that you really *see* me, a plea for me to act in your best interest. Tangible evidence that you understand my world and that you deserve so much more than what I've given you. Hermione and I have agreed these need to be incorporated in our next cycle."

"They're yours. I look forward to seeing them. I belong in a saddle."

"You can be both places, should you change your mind. Chloe—"

Hermione squeezed my mother's hand. "Now's the time, Brook. Without you, none of our circles are complete."

I glanced at Trout.

"Listen to your momma," he said.

"You were clearly done that day with Jeffrey. I should've trusted my gut and cut ties with him long before. I should've just been here for you like

I promised. When I saw this journal, I knew it was an invitation. Not an *opportunity* but an invitation. One I couldn't pass up."

"I agree. You should've walked away from him sooner. I trusted you. I believed in us."

She pulled a tattered cardboard jewelry box from her purse. She opened it and put on the faded macaroni necklace it held. "You made this for me. Do you remember? I wear it when I miss you. And that's a lot."

"Of course I remember. I can't believe you still have it." I touched the heart charm on the necklace I wore that she'd given me about the time I'd made the macaroni necklace.

"I came here today because I thought delivering your birthday present on time this year was more important than ever. I love you, Chloe Jean McIntyre."

I'd promised myself I wouldn't shed any more tears over my momma. I turned on a heel and went inside when the quiver rose from my belly. I wiped wetness from the corners of my eyes. The voices on the porch went silent. I stood at the fireplace with my back to the door and stared at the picture of Hermione and Trout. We all had circles. The circle I had with my mother had been broken many times. The circle Trout had with Hermione had been broken too, but they were proof that circles could be mended. I held the heart charm on my necklace and squeezed. I'd worn it every day for a reason, and the reason was standing outside, on Trout's porch.

I'd already proven that spending years apart from someone I loved only created a void, a void that only my mother could fill. I walked to the front door and peered through the screen. Hermione consoled my mother. Her gaze met mine with the creak of the hinges.

Emotion flowed through me with the hitch in my breath. Keeping my feelings at bay was no longer an option. Victory and hardship were bosom buddies whether I wanted them to be or not. It was time to accept my mother was human—and so was I.

"The thing is, you can't see the breaks in a circle. You can't see where it begins and where it ends. And some circles are complicated and lopsided." My big toe broke through the sole of my boot as I shuffled closer to my mom. I leaned against the railing and inspected the hole in the leather. "Well, I guess you could call this a sign, maybe even perfect timing."

"What are you gonna do, kid?" Trout scratched his whiskers.

"Put on the studded pair of boots back at the house."

Mom clasped her hands over her heart.

"Mom, I can't do what we've been through again, and cutting you off at the pass won't always be possible."

"Cutting me off at the pass isn't a burden you need to carry. You inspire me to do better. I've learned about boundaries the hard way. I couldn't bear losing you for good. Instead of inventing ways into your life, I'll simply ask from now on. I believe in us, too." Mom straightened her shoulders.

"I don't want to lose you either. I don't need things from you except those boots because I've been too stubborn to buy new ones. All I need is you, and simply asking would be lovely." I melted into her embrace and squeezed her so hard, she squealed. "I love you, Mom. I always have, and I always will."

After hugging my mom, I turned to Trout. "We about done here, cowboy? Me and my momma have some catching up to do."

"My circle begins and ends with you, kid."

"I've been thinking about that chapter book you loaned me. The boy learned an important lesson. Sometimes bad things bring good outcomes, like today. Timing is everything, but you already know that. And you're not gonna like what's coming next."

"I can take anything you can dish out."

"You sure about that?" I stepped closer to him.

"Nope." The apples of his cheeks held a smile.

He opened his arms, and I fell into them like I did my grandpa's after a day of learning hard lessons. Trout smelled like the cigarettes he carried in the red box, leather, and everything I loved about my grandpa.

Trout and I had exhausted our words. There wasn't anything more we needed to say. I turned to Hermione. Her dark hair flowed over her shoulders, her turquoise jewelry and smile as earthy and beautiful as the heritage of her people.

"We have many circles, Chloe." She took my hands in hers. The circle tattoo on the inside of her wrist was faded like the picture of her and Trout.

"I suppose we do," I said. "Welcome to the ranch. Trout leaves the key under the mat for me. Guess I should knock from now on."

Trout laughed and put his arm around Hermione. "I've missed you, woman."

"Come on, Mom. We'll walk Gypsy home. You can meet Maria, and thanks for calling her. The girls will be glad to see you."

CHAPTER 23

ONCE THE FLAG was thrown, the antics between Tristan and me would end. Today, I would run free on the back of my best girl. Would Lil and Gracie mind if I called Gypsy my best girl now that they were on the scene?

I braided my hair, put on my silver necklace with the heart charm, patted my cheeks, and gave myself a pep talk. "You're gonna whop him, fair and square," I said. *I hope.* I pointed to myself in the mirror. "You *will* whop him."

Matt called to me from the kitchen. He'd gotten up early, changed the babies, and made me breakfast. The aroma of bacon wafted upstairs. The tables had turned, and I dug being doted on.

I'd managed to fit into my favorite pair of jeans. I threaded Grandpa's belt through the belt loops and smoothed down the white blouse with the slubby embroidery Mom had given me. I inspected the tips of my studded boots that I'd buffed before bed last night.

Matt called for me to eat my breakfast again,

and I hustled downstairs. Gracie and Lil were seated in their carriers next to the table atop the carrier stands Maria suggested we buy to save our backs. Matt greeted me with a bouquet of wildflowers. I smiled at the stem of thistle he'd bound so the thorns wouldn't be prickly.

"My favorite. Thank you. You're awfully sweet." I kissed Matt's cheek then sat down at the table.

"Good to have you back." He placed the flowers in a vase and set it on the table before joining me.

"Didn't know I'd gone anywhere. How do you like your new home? You can always move back to the bunkhouse if us girls are too much for you."

"Justin and Tristan gave me a week. Silas and Quinn wished me luck and sent me on my way."

I laughed, devoured two strips of bacon, then ate my oatmeal and sliced banana. I inspected the backside of the toast.

"It's not burnt. I'll teach you how to cook, Momma."

"You've been holding out on me. Did the babies eat?" I reached across Gracie to tickle Lil's toes. "I guess that's a silly question since they're not crying. Feeding them formula is making a difference. I like your headbands, little girls. A bandanna never goes out of style." I checked my back pocket for the bandanna embroidered with Ida May's initials I'd wear for the race.

"Good morning, Gracie May. Gladiola predicted your eyes would be green as Irish fields, and she was right." While rubbing Gracie's belly, she grabbed my finger. "You're mighty strong."

"Like her momma. Now finish your breakfast. We've got a race to get to."

Sun streamed through the open window. The lace curtains billowed above the sink, catching messages from the valley. "Listen," I told the girls, pointing to the window. They both stopped wiggling and their eyes grew wide. "Can you hear them?"

Matt smiled and sipped his coffee.

"It's Winston and Ida May." The breeze kissed my cheek. "Your great-grandpa was the best cowboy ever. He brought me here. They say I favor Ida May—she was a force to be reckoned with, too. Your grandpa will tell you her stories." I spread huckleberry jam on my toast and took a bite. "You two little ladies must be special 'cause your daddy and I are sure they brought you home."

"The Lord works in mysterious ways," Matt said.

"Yes, He does," I replied. When the curtains settled back into place, the girls fussed. "Oh boy, here we go. Is the wagon hitched up?"

"Yep. Glad's ready for the ride. She's been spouting off about this for a week now. Maria will be here soon to help with the girls."

"Steaks on the grill and all the fixings later on. Can't wait." I fed Lil the rest of her bottle while I finished the last few bites of my breakfast.

"You're getting to be a pro at that." Matt finished his coffee.

Lil gummed the nipple and fell asleep. "Guess she wasn't hungry after all."

"She wanted your attention. I can understand why." Matt stood to clear the table.

Gracie's cheeks turned beet red. We waited for the shriek, and when it came, we laughed.

"This one's a firecracker." I handed Matt my empty bowl and silverware.

"Definitely like your momma," he said, touching his nose to hers.

"Yes, just like me."

Gracie May stared at me as if she were listening to breaking news. She kicked her legs, and I swear if she could have, she would have taken her first steps right then and there.

"I know, little girl, but you'll walk in your own

time." Her eyelids grew heavy, and I held her tiny hand until she conked out. "I'm heading to the barn. Do you need any help packing the girls' bag?"

"Nope."

"I knew you could do it." I gave him a thumbs-up.

"You did it last night," Matt said.

"I know."

"Get out of here, before crazy happens. Gypsy's waiting."

"Have Hermione and my mother gotten here?"

"They're at Trout's with Glad. Justin and I will swing by with the wagon and pick them up."

GYPSY AND I met Tristan and Casanova at the starting line. Glad waved from the wagon as Justin, Quinn, Silas, and Dad, all riding their favorite rides, trotted to the finish line. Trout watched on at the midway point.

"May the better person win," I said.

Tristan nodded. His quiet, competitive nature and steely gaze sent a shiver down my spine. He thrived on stoic emotion. Sun stroked his strong jaw. We all had somebody with wings watching over us. Vivian spoke to him the way Grandpa and

Ida May spoke to me. I hugged Gypsy's neck. She'd never tire of me clinging to her. Her shallow breaths were quick and steady. She purred and swished her tail. "We got this, girl." I held the reins loosely. This was her show. I was just an accessory. Mom said accessories made design shine.

Matt neared with a trophy in hand. The tall grass brushed against his shins. His white cowboy hat shaded his handsome face. When the clouds drifted past, the light shone upon him like the beacon he was.

His gaze met mine. There were no smiles. This was business.

"That's the trophy? You've got to be kidding. The horse doesn't have any legs," I said.

"That's because coming in second wasn't your strong suit growing up. I couldn't find any horse trophies intact in that box I took to the attic the day you moved in." He read the engraved plaque. "Summer Hill Rodeo. Bronco Division. Second Place."

"I like it," Tristan said. "It's unique. One-of-a-kind, just like you."

I tied my bandanna around my head. "Let's get this throw down started." I glanced over to the wagon. Glad and Maria had front row seats, holding the girls. Mom and Hermione stood next to the horses, their stances mirroring each other. The courage they'd harnessed to complete their circles illuminated their intent gazes.

From the corner of my eye, I peeked at Tristan. The creases framing his gaze caught the light when he winked. Casanova's muscles twitched. "Eye on the prize," Tristan said in a slow, deep tone.

I eyed Quinn, waiting for him to drop the flag. Adrenaline rippled through me like the chill of an autumn morning. "No nerves," I uttered. Gypsy craned her neck to see me, her striking profile dark as night. She was ready to run. She had my back, and I had hers.

Gypsy pawed at the ground. Matt rested his right hand on her chest and his left hand on Casanova's. Matt glanced at Tristan, then to me. A thin smile tugged at Matt's lip. Tristan and I nodded.

Quinn sat tall on his paint, Chaplin, and raised the white flag.

I rubbed the silver heart hanging around my neck. Quinn dropped the flag, and I slapped Gypsy's rump with the reins. "Ya!" I yelled.

Hooves of thunder beat the ground. Gypsy and Casanova ran neck and neck until Casanova took the lead. With another slap of the reins and a heel kick, I placed my pinky and pointer fingers between my teeth and let out a piercing whistle. Gypsy hung steady but only for a moment. She pulled away in the next five strides.

I didn't look back.

Focused on the finish line, Gypsy ran faster than she ever had. Her mane thrashed, and she grunted to reach a goal I couldn't fathom. I crouched low and whispered to her even though she couldn't hear me. "Come on, girl. You can do it." I flicked the reins against her shoulders. From the corner of my eye, I saw Casanova close in. Too scared to breathe, I gave Gypsy one more kick, and we flew across the finish line.

"Run, girl, run." The breeze cooled my cheeks, and exhilaration cleared my mind as we chased the never-ending horizon. When Gypsy eased up, I glanced back at my family. "You're right, girl. Running away sounds like a great idea sometimes until you realize you've left behind the people who love you most."

In the distance, my mother cheered me on. Goose bumps covered my arms. "Actions shouldn't outshine words, and words shouldn't outshine our actions. I'll remember that when I'm raising the girls."

Gypsy reared up and slapped at the air with her

hooves. "Woohoo!" I shouted, stroking her damp hide. Gypsy whinnied and circled back toward Casanova and Tristan.

"Looks like you're having fun." Tristan's hard stare dissolved.

"I am. Good ride, cowboy." Sweat trickled down my back, and I adjusted the bandanna on my brow. Loose strands of hair brushed my cheeks.

"I'll get you next time," Tristan replied.

We dismounted and shook hands.

"I look forward to it. We should get a real trophy though." The corners of his mouth lifted as he took in the majestic Montana sky. "You're wearing a mighty big grin for a loser," I said.

"There are no losers here." Tristan whispered to Casanova.

"What are you telling him?"

Tristan clicked his tongue against his teeth and tapped Casanova on the shoulder. "Come on, boy. Bow."

With one knee to the ground, Casanova bowed his head to me, then got back up on all fours.

"If you'd lost, we wouldn't have been able to do that," Tristan said.

"Amazing."

Tristan clicked his tongue, tapped Gypsy on the shoulder, and spoke to her in a deep, gentle tone.

"Down, Gypsy. Bow." She bowed to Casanova and got back up.

"When?" I asked.

Tristan's lowered gaze didn't dim the glimmer in his eyes. "That's not all she can do. While you were out of commission, I taught her a few more tricks."

I met her stare head-on. "What else did he teach you, girl?"

Tristan took sugar from his pocket and held it above her snout. Gypsy showed him her teeth, then held up her front leg like a dog to shake. Tristan patted her shin, then fed her the treat.

"I hope Maggie's getting this," I said.

Casanova showed me his teeth, then ate sugar from Tristan's hand, too.

"So this is why you talked me into feeding them carrots. Now you're the guy with the sugar. Remember, a little bit goes a long way."

"I'll whop you next time," Tristan said.

"Just because you can sweet-talk my horse doesn't mean you can sweet-talk me," I quipped.

Matt shook his head. "I told you not to show Chloe what you taught Gypsy. It'll only spur my girl on."

Tristan laughed and nudged me with his shoulder.

"You should let yourself run wild more often.

It's good for the soul," I said.

Tristan kicked at the ground. "Maybe so, Chloe McIntyre. Maybe so." He put his hand on the back of my neck and gave it a gentle squeeze. "I've ridden with the best of them, and none of them come close to you."

"That's a mighty big compliment, Tristan Donoghue. Between the two of us, we can tame this wild Montana land if we put our minds to it."

"I bet we could." He slapped his leather gloves against his thigh.

"But if you did, then what would be left for the rest of us?" Matt rubbed his stubbly chin.

I fingered the silver charm skimming my collarbone. It didn't possess anything magical to grant the wishes I'd made. It represented the faith I'd carried with me even when I thought I'd had none left.

I wrapped my arms around Gypsy's neck, and she rested her head on my shoulder. I was where I needed to be. "All roads lead home," I told her.

Matt cupped his hands and hoisted me into the saddle. I threw my leg over and settled in. The breeze kicked up and kissed the nape of my neck. I looked toward Grandpa's memorial on the distant ridge, blew him a kiss, circled Matt, and galloped toward home.

The Montana Bred journey continues with...

Showdown, Montana Bred, Book 3

When big dreams lead to self-discovery and purpose, Chloe McIntyre must face her fears to accept forever love.

To learn more about *Showdown* ...

FOLLOW ME:

Linda's Website & Newsletter:
www.lindabradleyauthor.com
Linda's Amazon Author Page: amzn.to/3rzhA1G
Facebook: LBradleyAuthor
BookBub: bookbub.com/profile/linda-bradley
Instagram: lindabradleyauthor
Twitter: @LBradleyAuthor
Goodreads:
goodreads.com/author/show/6498473.Linda_Bradley

Reviews and recommendations are much appreciated and can be submitted on Amazon, BookBub, or Goodreads.

NOTE TO READERS

Dear Reader,

Thank you for reading *Reunion*. The characters of the 617 Ranch hold a special place in my heart, as do readers like you!

Should you select one of my books for your book club and would like to invite me to a meeting, email me at LBradley@LindaBradleyAuthor.com. Please write BOOK CLUB in the subject line. Let me know a bit about your group, how many members you have, where you meet, and which book you've read. We can meet via cyberspace or in person, should you live local to me. If I don't respond, please reach out on social media. Glitches sometimes happen.

Feel free to send me a photo. I love seeing my books being read in a favorite place.

Thanks again for picking up a copy of *Reunion*. I look forward to sharing *Showdown*, book 3 of the *Montana Bred Series* with you!

Sincerely,
Linda Bradley

LINDA'S BOOKS

Unbranded (Montana Bred Series Book 1)

Threatened by the unexpected, devoted rancher—
Chloe McIntyre refuses to compromise her
ambition or her legacy.

Maggie's Way
(Montana Bound Series Book 1)

Middle-aged Maggie Abernathy just wants to
recuperate from cancer, but when Chloe and John
McIntyre move in next door, somehow her empty
house becomes home again.

Maggie's Fork in the Road
(Montana Bound Series Book 2)

Just when Maggie Abernathy thinks she's got her
life in order, she faces loss and makes an
unexpected friendship.

Maggie's Montana
(Montana Bound Series Book 3)

Maggie Abernathy makes good on a promise that changes her life forever.

A Montana Bound Christmas: Ho, Ho, Home for the Holidays!
(Montana Bound Series Book 4)

Unexpected guests and a lost dog bring the *Montana Bound Series* cast of misfits together for a special Montana Christmas.

The Montana Bound Series on Amazon:
amzn.to/3rzhA1G

The Montana Bred Series on Amazon:
amzn.to/3rzhA1G

More by Linda

Pedal

Can a whisper from beyond give middle-aged Paula Murphy, burdened by heartache, the courage to just pedal?

Coming back to her Bay View summer home in northern Michigan means more than planning picnics at the beach and working in her daughter-in-law's bicycle shop. Her avoidance to embrace her grown son's death isn't the only tribulation weighing on this self-reliant social worker's mind.

Reluctant to believe the unfathomable, Paula Murphy's world is turned upside down when she's reunited with the only man she's ever loved.

Pedal on Amazon: amzn.to/3rzhA1G

About the Author

 Linda's inspiration comes from her favorite authors and life itself. Her character-driven stories integrate humor found in everyday situations, family drama, and forever love. Her distinct voice creates memorable journeys and emotion.

Linda's been a finalist in the Booksellers Best Contest and Romance Reviews Readers' Choice Awards. She lives in Michigan with her artist husband, sons, and rescue dog. Linda loves art, animals, and stories with hope and heart.